Foreword

Overcoming adversaries

Do you have a bucket list? I do. I've always had a list of cool things that I wanted to be and do by the time Mr. Reaper comes for me. As a child I wanted to be rich and famous. I wanted to be an astronaut or pop star. I wanted to be popular and super muscly and be a superhero.

As a teenager I still had a bucket list but there were other things in the bucket that I just wanted. I still wanted to be popular but this time I really meant it. I also wanted to be muscly. I wanted to do well at school and be good at sports. I wanted to have true friends and self-confidence. I wanted to avoid the bullies that tormented me with comments and confrontation. I wanted to be able to avoid things in life that made me sad and I wanted to talk with people about these things but wasn't fully aware of them at that time of my life.

As an adult my bucket list was cast aside for many years in favour of my list of 'wants'. Whereas the bucket list should be achievement based, my list of 'wants' was avoidance based.

I still wanted self-esteem and friends. I also wanted to forget. I wanted to get rid of the feelings of worry and anxiety. I wanted to disappear. I wanted to understand why I wanted certain things and why I felt certain emotions. Sometimes I wanted to end it all. Sometimes I wanted to drive fast in a straight line regardless of the bends in the road or the legal speed limit of the law. I wanted to be free of debt but I wanted a fun life and a high standard of living. I wanted to be high as a kite but I wanted to be sober too. I wanted money and status because I hoped they would cover up true feelings of lack of self-worth.

At the current time of my life I am back with my bucket list as it should be and working on ticking things off and realising what I have overcome and accomplished in life rather than feeling overwhelmed by the stress and anxiety that modern living can throw at you.

Throughout my adult life I have made many wrong decisions that have taken me to extremely dark and low places. Poor financial decisions have caused me to end up bankrupt and without fixed abode. I would spend many months sleeping on the floors of charitable acquaintances before finding a room to rent in a single bedroom DSS flat.

Lack of self-esteem and individuality meant I made more poor decisions and succumbed to peer pressure. This lead me to smoking and drugs and I would eventually lose many years of progress to a full time habit that all but took over my waking hours.

I had always been troubled by what I consider a complete abandonment by my birth father from when I was young. Two failed attempts to rekindle a relationship with him would further scar my personality and leave me with a glitch in my persona meaning that I would expect people to eventually abandon me just like he did.

Eventually my mind decided it had taken all that it could take and that I had spent long enough living with buried demons and stress and it decided to take some time off from work. I had a breakdown and was diagnosed as clinically depressed. I spent a period of my life taking more drugs (prescribed this time) and floating in and out of counselling and even touching base on anger management.

There comes a time in everyone's life where you have a choice between embarking on a journey on one of two very different paths. On one side you can choose a path encased in a safety bubble that temporarily protects you from harm but that is a false security. It will eventually end and it will most certainly put your life on hold whilst you rest on the 'pause' button. The other path is a long and arduous journey that holds no promises, no guarantees and can only be trusted to take you to hell and beyond in order to reach your destination. Your *potential*.

With the help of loved ones and an internal burning need to succeed I made a conscious decision to turn things around in my life. I started to see the light at the end of the tunnel as daylight rather than an approaching train. Whilst the fire of positivity may become a tiny ember at some stages in life it is still burning and can be built up again if the desire and *motivation* is strong enough.

I have strived to overcome my demons and I continue to do this every day that I am alive. I thank God for what I have and what I am able to do rather than avoiding real life issues and stress. As time goes on I learn how to stride straight through the fields of fear and self-doubt rather than turning back to an easier option.

The one thing that was always there and that I often longed for throughout my troubled years was martial arts. The club and the self-induced penance of the training would always assist in cleansing my soul and making me realise that I was capable of more than I often realised.

This book recounts many of my thoughts and beliefs as I chose the long, arduous path towards black belt and hopefully serves as a mental reference to those who decide to take that same path for themselves. For those who make this choice, I commend you. I respect you. I wish you the very best because you are about to go on quite a journey my friend.

Chapter One
Karate

When you embark upon a journey remember that every step is important. Without each step you don't complete the journey.

"What the hell am I doing here?" has to be a question that lots of people have asked themselves when first stepping into the training hall for the first time. I know I did. When someone decides to take the long, scenic route to black belt their mind-set usually thinks one of two things. Some people embrace the ethos from their very first step into the hall. They are curious and open to instruction and learning yet have no apprehension of what lies ahead of them. No doubt that they are making the right choice. They are the warriors of this world. Sometimes people want to be warriors but are ignorant and just want to prove a system wrong. They either drop out or think they are a grandmaster after 6 months of lessons. But the warriors are the people who will follow their martial path for the rest of their lives without problem. They are born warriors. They know their white belt will eventually become a black belt. They are likely to be leaders and will be keen to learn, impress and progress. This warrior creed may comprise 10% of new starters (if that). For the rest of us, we ask that question of ourselves: "What the hell am I doing here?"- And so you should! To ask yourself why you do something is to explore the very reason for your desire to do it. If you are overweight and decide to lose weight you must ask yourself 'why do I want to lose weight?' There is no point in just doing something without a reason and you have a far greater chance of success if you can uncover the real reasons why you want to achieve an objective rather than just going in blind and hoping for the best. Always have a reason to remember to spur you on and revisit it. Often. You will need it many times before you tie a black belt around your waist.

I fell into this category. Having experienced a certain amount of bullying at school mixed with a certain natural lack of self-esteem I developed a slight phobia of confrontation; a phobia that would grow over the years to be a nemesis and yet also a catalyst to motivate me further.

I grew up in a small village in north Essex near to Saffron Walden. As a young child life was good. I feel privileged to have had a countryside upbringing and have fond memories of green views, fields and trees and exploring remote woods. I experienced nature at its best and had all the space and fresh air that a child needs to flourish and grow. It helped having an older brother too especially as we were similar sizes growing up. We had our battles like all brothers do but we helped each other along the way to adulthood.

My secondary school was 20 miles away and from the outset it was clear to see that I would have to work harder than most to make friends. At the age of 11 I went from being top dog in primary school to being bottom of the food chain in secondary school. I settled into a routine and in all honesty didn't find school too bad. I enjoyed the school work. I had a few friends. It was okay. But there were a few times when the bullies got the better of me. I specifically remember one incident where I was sitting on a wall at the edge of one of the four playgrounds next to the large playing fields. I think we were doing some sort of art class and were released into the school to draw something. I would have been around twelve years old. There were some older lads kicking a football around in this particular playground and, as I paused to watch them for a moment, the ball came over my way as one of them missed whatever he was aiming at. Now for most twelve year old boys this would not be a problem: just kick the ball back and carry on. Not for me though. I had never been what you would call 'gifted' when it came to the beautiful game and although my intent to return the ball was pure and true my aim was not. I kicked the ball and it skewed off in the wrong direction and past them.

This kick could probably be seen as a pivotal point in my life. For whatever reason, one of the lads took severe offence to my lack of skill, walked over to me and said in a low voice "you're gonna get it on the school bus tonight."

He was true to his word, which was probably the only genuine thing about him. That evening as I sat on the front seat of the school bus (yes the front seat), this sixth former edged his way from the back of the bus to the front whilst his mate went to sit next to my older brother to stop him intervening. In all honesty I don't think my brother could have done much. He wasn't inclined to fight any more than I was. I remember the sixth former ending up sitting on the seat adjacent to me across the bus aisle just staring at me. He was leaning forward towards me and looked like he was going to enjoy whatever he had planned for me. But he waited. I knew what was coming. He knew too. But he waited.

He waited for about a mile which felt like an eternity, just staring at me with as menacing a look as he could muster. Why was he waiting?!

He would have been about a foot or so taller than me and easily had a couple of stone in weight. I was twelve years old. He would have been sixteen. It was a complete mismatch and the reason for it was just ludicrous. I started shaking. My legs felt like jelly and I needed to go to the toilet. I wanted to run but couldn't and didn't have anywhere to go anyway. I didn't want to fight. I was more inclined to plead for my release. I sat there and waited for my fate with so many emotions running through my mind I couldn't think straight at all. I shot a glance at my brother, several seats back boxed in to his seat next to the window by another school thug.

The bus rounded the final corner to the long, straight road where my brother and I get dropped off at the driveway at the end of our house. As the bus slowed down enough for my angry nemesis to balance, he stood up and unleashed a flurry of punches as hard as he could on the top of my head. All I could do was cover my head in my hands and hope that I could sufficiently protect myself from harm. I couldn't run- the bus doors weren't open yet. It was probably ten seconds of my life that seemingly went on forever. I was alone with no way out and in no control over what was happening to me.

As the bus finally stopped and the doors opened, Dimwit the bus driver finally realised that something was afoot behind him and turned around at which point the pain in my hands and head eased for a moment as my attacker decided he had taught me enough of a lesson. Maybe he hoped I would take up football lessons in case I ever needed to pass the ball back to someone in future. I shakily got up, wholly oblivious to whether anyone actually cared enough to ask me if I was alright. Fear and adrenaline had temporarily taken control of my body and I wobbled down the stairs of the bus. My brother walked me into the house. He must've felt bad for me seeing as he couldn't have done anything to help but it really wasn't his fault. Mum knew immediately that something had happened and as my brother told her I looked at my hands which were now turning black and blue from where I had protected myself. There were some choice lumps appearing on my head too.

I was horrified.

I couldn't believe that this sort of thing happened to people. I hadn't done anything to deserve this and while my family erupted in anger around me I just stared at my colourful, shaking hands with wide eyes of disbelief and self-pity.

From there, my step dad decided this was bang out of order. This lad lived on an army barracks on the other side of the village and he drove me straight down there to demand that something be done. A lot of the army children went to my primary and secondary school. Some would stay for the whole of their education whilst other would come and go as their parents were shipped to other barracks or countries to serve as required. It must have been hard on some of the kids who would have preferred a more stable life rather than moving around. This lad was apparently the son of a major and as my step dad angrily told the gate staff and with automatic weapons what had

9

happened we were reassured that he would be 'dealt with'. I never saw him again. Apparently he had been expelled that day for dealing drugs on school premises and he had decided to take his anger out on me. Ironically though, once he had started hitting me I had felt a slight alleviation of the intense feeling of fear that had built up inside me. The anticipation of what was imminently about to happen on the school bus that day was far worse than the actual incident itself. That was my first lesson in dealing with fear: having an unexpected adrenaline rush and dealing with the pre-fight nerves and emotions and then also, dealing with the aftermath. I had developed fear in a way that I had never experienced before. Fear of confrontation tinged with fear of being hurt. I was embarrassed that I couldn't protect myself. I was ashamed that I could do nothing to save face in front of people who would spread the news around school like wildfire the next day (even though mobile phones weren't around then). I had lost control of a part of my personality and self-confidence through no choice of my own and was having to navigate dealing with my fragile state of mind and changing behaviour. No one had given me a map though.

That boy's name was Matt. If I met Matt today I would feel no malice towards him. I would forgive him and shake his hand (unless he turned out be a complete fuckwit or axe murderer or something). That was a pivotal moment in my life that encouraged me to embark on a method to overcome that type of situation ever happening again. And it wasn't taking football lessons. I would also ask him to put on a pair of 4oz gloves, gum shield and groin guard and step into a cage with me. I don't know whether he is 20 stone of muscle or lard, fit or fat, hard or soft. I don't know whether he is skilled in combat through lesson or through the street. He may have fought in the army or on a Friday night in the local boozer after a skin full. I don't know whether he turned out to be a thoroughly bloody decent chap. I don't give a shit. I've fought big guys and won and I've fought small guys who have handed my arse to me on a plate but I never back down from a fair fight if there is a point to it. I would just want the chance to see what would happen now the odds are fairer. Now *that's* a fight that I don't mind losing.

The ability to realise that I was afraid of fighting and violence also allowed me to discover a reason as to why I wanted to overcome said fear. I had a choice to ignore it and remain in the shadows ever to be afraid of whoever might look at me the wrong way or be a potential threat to my safety. Or I could deal with it head on. I am so glad I chose to deal with it.

So when you step foot inside that dojo for the first time and say to yourself "why the hell am I here?" it is a decent and just question. I asked myself and I am glad that I had a good answer. I have never forgotten the reason why I train: motivation.

A couple of years passed in between that incident and my first experience of martial arts and daytime white pyjamas. A girlfriend of mine (equally as picked on at school as me) quickly heard about the incident and said to me one lunch time "why don't you go to the multi gym?" I didn't know what a multi gym was. I went to ask the games staff about this and was told that the 'multi gym' was open for use at lunchtimes. (This was before lots of health and safety rules came into play that made teachers realise it was actually really fucking stupid to allow kids to use weights as they pleased).

So I went to the 'multi gym'.

My school was built on the same ground as Dunmow Sports Centre which meant we had quite amazing access to facilities that other schools did not: on site swimming pool, squash courts, tennis courts, basketball courts and more. The multi gym was good. It had enough stations to train all major muscle parts and after a play around I realised what it was about and became hooked. This machine enabled people to grow their muscles beyond the power of normal puberty and I had access to it for free. This was an opportunity. I needed to make the most of this.

11

For the next couple of years I visited the multi gym as often as I could. I read magazines like Flex and Muscle & Fitness and put together a folder of exercises and routines. I cut out pictures of the greats of the era: Arnold, Tom Platz, Dorian Yates, Mike Mattarazzo. I made a visual motivational reference tool of what to do and how to do it. I had calorie charts and all sorts. I devised all my own workouts. In hindsight they were not well chosen routines as I was trying to emulate huge bodybuilders so my routines were designed for professional bodybuilders rather than teenage stick insects. But the sheer effort that I put in mixed with a huge natural release of teenage hormones seemed to work. I trained at school and trained at home with a few weights that I bought. I got bigger. Not Schwartzeneggar big but I looked pretty good. I trained to look bigger so that I wouldn't be picked on. I wanted muscle to act as a visual deterrent. But I still got picked on.

I found mental bullying as bad as physical bullying. Affecting the mind-set of someone has a massive effect on their physical ability. Emotion and mind-set can win or lose a fight before a physical action has even occurred. This was enough to keep reminding me that I had this nagging gremlin in my head that kept saying *"hey, you remember when that guy beat the crap out of you in front of everyone? You remember? You cleverly curled up in a ball so you couldn't see or defend yourself and got beaten up anyway? I bet you couldn't defend yourself now too! I bet you'd get beaten up again. You don't know how to fight! You might be a bit stronger but you can't fight! You don't know how! You're just a slightly bigger loser now."*

Saffron Walden was my local town. It has a population of around 14,000 when I was young and was a quaint town situated in the north of Essex. It has a certain amount of night life which catered to those who liked alternative, rock and heavy metal music.

My first evening out was in Saffron Walden and I was feeling way out of my comfort zone I can tell you. I was fifteen years old and with a few friends from the village where I lived. We were waiting to hear one of the local bands play at the Walden Club. I don't know whether I had a slightly sheltered childhood living in the country but I would strongly suggest that I was behind on being 'streetwise' and 'savvy' on the social scene. I was shy and quiet in groups especially if people were confident and outgoing.

The Walden Club was situated on the High Street of Saffron Walden and on this particular night there was a local grungy rock band playing who would attract many interestingly clothed people. By this time I had grown my hair long and only wore black clothes, mostly with rips on and in support of choice bands like Nirvana, Pearl Jam or Guns n Roses. We were the Grungers- a minority in our school outnumbered by the 'ravers' of the time. I found our alternative group more in tune to their emotions and open to deep discussion and equally deep friendships than other people who I knew.

As we waited outside the front of the Club on the high street waiting for a few of the guys to turn up from another town I heard some shouting across the street. I couldn't quite work out where it was coming from so I crossed the road to find out. There was a small alleyway in between a couple of the shops that I had never noticed before. Why would I? It led to the local scout hut up a thin flight of wooden stairs. The shouting was coming from through a window above the door. It wasn't random shouting though. The people were shouting together as a group, deliberately and making the same kind of sound: '*hiyaaaaa!*' It was the *kiai*: a shout to release the energy in a technique whilst tensing the core to improve power. It was synonymous with karate and once I figured it out my curiosity was raised to a level that meant I would not be satisfied until I had experienced what this class had to offer.

A couple of weeks later with a lot of nervous energy and eager anticipation I stepped through that door in the alley way and into a dark, wooden room with a lot of men who I thought were invincible and amazing and putting on these white suits and colourful belts. I didn't have any white pyjamas yet and tried to look normal as the men changed and discussed life and martial arts and occasionally nodded in my direction as a sign of acceptance.

I joined the back of the queue as they filed up the stairs and through a wooden door into a wooden floored room with bare walls and not enough light. The windows were small, single pane and dirty with cobwebs. There was no pretence in this room. No luxury. Just a very stout man with a faded black belt tied around his waist waiting for us to organise ourselves and line up. He had noticed me because our eyes had met momentarily before I looked away in fear. I was sure he frowned at my very presence. He didn't speak. He didn't smile. He just told us to 'hurry up'. I was ushered to the far left of the line of students and everyone fell silent waiting for the lesson to begin.

I said to myself: "what the hell am I doing here?"

This was *Shotokan* Karate as founded by the late Gichin Funakoshi from Japan. I didn't realise at that age that there are many styles of karate as well as various other martial arts too. I didn't know any different. I had heard of karate and all of the clichés that came with it: the karate chop, breaking bricks, the white pyjamas and being invincible. This was the early 90s and things were a little different back then, especially in a small town environment.

In the last 20 years there has been more off shoot martial arts popping up than ever before. Imagine all the main martial arts being grouped together in a ball and then that ball exploding into a hundred pieces- each piece has some usefulness. The bigger the piece the more martial knowledge included but there are also lots of smaller pieces that don't have much to offer. This is how martial arts work now. It is a minefield and there are too many useless off shoot styles to mention here. What usually happens is, some Joe studies a martial art for a while thinking they will be a warrior within a year. They learn something but feel they know enough long before they realise that they are still a novice. Often these people reach black belt so please don't think that doing an exam and earning this coveted piece of equipment means that you are the next Bruce Lee because it won't without being tied around the right person with the right work ethic and attitude. They take their black belt, leave the proper tutelage of their instructor and set up their own style often promoting themselves up to a high black belt level to invoke credibility. Over the years these types of schools have been called McDojos. Incapable instructors hide behind flashy training halls and false flattery and often won't let their students compete outside of their own school or association for fear of being shown for the charlatans that they are. Sometimes they even say they won't compete because they train to kill! Makes you wonder how they train, doesn't it?!

It is prudent to check out a style before committing yourself to a school. Have you heard of the style before? Will the instructor show you their credentials and certificates? Are they part of a governing body? Are they offended if you ask them who gave them their black belt? These are all important questions to ask. For example, Chinese styles will often quote their lineage back to the founder of a style and therefore the less number of people back to the original founder, the purer the art form should be. I had an MMA instructor once who teaches Hop Gar Kung Fu and is the 3rd generation from the grandmaster. I would rather be taught by him than someone 7th or 8th down the line. That's not

15

to say both these instructors can't be good but it is about percentages. National governing bodies can be checked out online. Is the association a proper international organisation or can you flush it out as a one man band who set up on his own and farmed some schools out to his loyal 'black belts'?

Bear in mind if you learn from one of these off shoot organisations you may be paying over the odds for inferior information and tuition. Do not be flattered by luxurious training venues and shiny white suits with lots of badges all over them. Do not be afraid to cross train at other schools. My Taekwon-Do instructor *never* minded if I trained with another school. He had nothing to prove and everything to give. I would always return to him as I found that he provided the best tuition. Other schools didn't seem to train as hard as our school. They wouldn't break boards at all. They wouldn't spar very often. These things were part of the syllabus so I couldn't understand why they wouldn't get covered in lesson. I didn't get a good feel from them. Most of all I respected my instructor more for letting me go and try. If an instructor forbids you from training with another school or style then what does this tell you? If they say it is because their school/ style is the best they are deluded. It is not. The martial art is only as effective as the martial artists that practice it. Cross training is beneficial. It is not rude or disrespectful. You are investing in your own safety and will quickly learn that no one style is 100% effective for self-defence. I once went to a Taekwon-Do class when mine was not on on that particular evening. The instructor came up to me after the class and said that if I could only return if I did not train at my other class. He said this was because I would get confused studying with two teachers or two styles. MMA students reading this book may fall about on the floor laughing at this stage and I join you wholeheartedly. I had enough respect for him as my senior grade not to question him but I also had the intelligence to know that he was being unreasonable and had an unnecessarily inflated ego. I don't need people like that around me. I have always returned to my original Taekwon-Do instructor throughout the years no matter where I have lived. When you find one that works for you, stay there. Just stay.

Shotokan karate is an offensive martial art comprised of strong, rigid stances and long, often straight movements. When I say offensive I mean that it is an external martial art designed to evade or block an attack and retaliate accordingly. Internal or soft styles concentrate more on energy within the body and improving health for the self. Examples could be Tai Chi, Chi Gung or Yoga. It can sometimes be hard for a beginner to choose a style of martial art because they might not know the difference between them. Karate, Kung Fu, Kick Boxing and all the others just elicit thoughts of old martial arts movies and some people might not think it even matters what style they chose. It is worth doing a little research on what you are looking to accomplish and then trying a few schools out. For example, Karate, Taekwon-do, kick boxing and Muay Thai are all stand up arts that use kicking, punching, blocking and evading. Japanese Jiu Jitsu covers take downs and ground work. Aikido covers takedowns too and loads of joint locks and manipulations. Judo covers takedowns and groundwork (especially Kodan Judo). Brazilian Jiu Jitsu predominantly covers groundwork. Escrima is stick fighting. Boxing is punching. There are big differences between fighting standing up, on the ground and with a weapon. It would therefore be obvious that you choose which range you want to major in before trying a Taekwon-Do class and expecting to wrestle or grapple.
Then of course there's MMA for those that can't make their mid up and just want to smash everyone using any means necessary. This particular class was run by *Sensei* (teacher), a 4th dan black belt. Sensei was in his mid to late 40s at this time. He was

stocky and had hard features. His eyes were narrow and small and you couldn't make out exactly where he looked or what colour his eyes were. His face was weathered with life and experience and sat under a short nest of wiry, grey hair. It was rare for Sensei to express any emotion. I don't know whether this was because of the environment that he was trying to create or just his natural disposition but as a 15 year old novice I certainly didn't want to upset him. He looked like he could flip his lid at any minute and I didn't want to find out what would happen if he did. He was the main man. At that time I believed he was the answer to all my problems too.

I was wrong.

This particular Shotokan class followed a syllabus that was mostly made up of *kata*. Kata are pre-arranged sequences of movements against a number of imaginary opponents and are designed to test an individual in memory, skill and ability. Many martial arts will have kata. I still practice some today. Kata form a way of assisting a student in a way of learning and a teacher or examiner in assessing groups of students. They can be an excellent workout and often as a student progresses through the ranks they will learn new moves by learning the *bunkai* or application of movements. I do not believe, however, that they are the only form of learning in martial arts.

Kata are pre-arranged movements so there is a strong sense of remembering specific sequences. Real fights won't work this way. Kata involve attacks and blocks to air. Nothing was actually hit or blocked which is not realistic. To experience contact is important. It feels different to hitting air and will evoke a different response in your body and also your opponent. Take for example a simple front kick/ punch combination. Many martial arts will have you performing movements up and down the training hall. Often a kick is followed by a punch. A simple technique is a front kick followed by a reverse punch. If you kick an opponent in the stomach, would you then follow up with a punch to his head? Although this sequence is often practised at a basic level, if your front kick actually contacts your attacker as it is meant to it is likely that they will either double over forward in pain from a snapping kick motion or be projected backwards from a pushing or thrusting motion. It is unlikely they will remain stock still so that you can follow up with your punch. After your front snap kick, maybe a knee to the head would be better as their head is already in the right place? These questions will arise time and time again in your journey to black belt and I have never grown tired of asking these questions of my masters. I now have to answer them too so I am glad I have some more answers now!

There was only 1 black belt in the class. He was a postman. The Postman was a bit bigger and taller than everyone else. I thought he was amazing. He stood at the far right of the class and could do all these strange looking kata which seemed to have hundreds of movements that made no sense at all. His kiai was loud and rumbled through the hall. I imagined being hit by The Postman would probably be akin to being hit by Thor's hammer. The Postman was invincible. He had to be- he had a black belt in karate. I wanted to be like The Postman.

Looking back, I realise how wrong I was. For around two years I diligently followed Sensei's instruction and learned my kata and pre-arranged block/ counter combos. We trained twice a week in loyal obedience. We did what was asked of us, didn't speak until given permission and tried harder and harder because nothing seemed to elicit any form of praise from Sensei. In 20 months I progressed from white belt to purple belt. Brown belt was next and then black after that. But nothing had changed in my mind. Why wasn't I starting to feel invincible? Maybe all that stuff falls into place when you get your black belt but I was sure something should have changed by now. Some of my peers held themselves with a confidence and strength that was not felt by myself so I invented a front that I used to exude confidence when I needed it. I tried to mimic the mannerisms and characteristics of those whom I admired. I thought this would be the way forward and was maybe a method of actually becoming the confident and strong person that I so badly wanted to be.

In the September of 1996 I packed up my things and headed off to university in Bedford. Within the first week I was looking for a karate class but try as I might I couldn't find one. About half a mile from my halls was a sports centre which I guessed would be a good place to enquire. I headed down there and went into reception. There was a notice board opposite the entrance doors and I went over to have a look. Two notices caught my eye: one was for Wing Chun Kung Fu and the other was for Taekwon-Do. Having no knowledge of either and cheesed off that I could not find my beloved Shotokan anywhere (there were three separate Shotokan classes in Bedford at that time- I just couldn't find them) I tossed a coin to see which one I would try. Taekwon-Do came out as the favoured choice and a few days later I returned to the sports centre to try the class out.

The class was held on the indoor running track of the sports hall. This was a bit different to what I was used to. There were women and children in this class. They wore white pyjamas too but they had cool oriental writing on the back with the word 'Taekwon-Do' across the top. The belts seemed different colours too. The instructor was a chap called Steve. Not Sensei. Steve. He came up to me and offered his fist to knock. I was used to bowing and only saying the word '*Oss*' in my last class (a respect word that seemed to mean everything). But here I was introducing myself to this friendly chap and telling him why I was here.

It was a good situation in a lot of ways. Here I was just starting university with all the time in the world to invest in my training. I had desire and youth well on my side.

That first lesson was an experience in fitness. Steve had us put through our paces in a way that I had not experienced in my two years of Shotokan. I had spent my karate years learning techniques. Now I'm not saying that is wrong- when you go to a martial arts class you are, in essence, paying your hard earned money for expert tuition in a form of combat. My technical experience was of a somewhat stiff and always pre-meditated nature though, It didn't flow and there was minimal realism involved.

If you simply wanted to be put through your paces on a regular basis you could join a gym and have some upstart tell you to push harder or faster and beast you till you despise them. But the benefits of fitness in martial arts should not be overlooked- indeed it should be embraced. Like me, many people start learning a martial art for the purpose of self-defence. That is a fine and decent reason to practice a martial art. However many will agree that the self-defence side of martial arts will compromise a lower percentage of the time you invest compared to fitness and efficacy of technique. Self-defence is about being able to protect yourself against some form of real attack if you were forced into that situation. You could, if you wanted, go to a self-defence course and learn what you needed to learn technically. You *should* be able to walk out of a self-defence lesson and be able to apply what you have learned straight away if required. Martial arts is different in that it will require you to commit to an investment in your time to learn to use it to your benefit. Don't think once you have taken your first grading there is something that amazingly sets you apart from the general populace. If you start developing an attitude that says '*Actually I'm pretty hard now cos I passed my first grading so don't mess with me or you'll get fucked up before you even realise it*', then you've got it wrong. This shit takes time. By all means invest in a self-defence course at the same time if you want but pure self-defence is something different. I believe it is more to do with

21

situation awareness and state of mind than hours of physically demanding lessons.

The other thing that martial arts offer is a way to get fit whilst applying what you are learning. The combat and sparring side of martial arts is a decent workout. You will likely learn techniques to improve flexibility and conditioning, how to build stronger, leaner muscles, how to control weight and that's just the physical side of the arts. The longer you learn and study the more you may develop psychologically. You may develop a different attitude towards your life. You might learn to appreciate what you have more, be more humble or become more ambitious. Martial arts will affect people in different ways and usually for the better. It is rare to find a high grade martial artist who is a bully or without moral integrity. You can rest assured you will be surrounding yourself with people who are on a similar journey as yourself and will be working not just on fitness and defence but becoming better people in general- and that is encouraging for all.

That first lesson in Taekwon-Do was just a normal lesson for Steve's regular students. I mean it wasn't anything special or different just because I was there but I found it physically demanding because it wasn't what I was used to. I had come from a small dusty wooden scout hut where we would spend our time practicing drills, pre-arranged attacks and defences in set stances and kata. That was it. There was no other aspect to those two years of training. I loyally followed Sensei's instructions and waited for the secret enlightenment that would transform me into the invincible warrior that I was expecting which of course didn't happen because guess what? I never sparred or did any training with realism.

My Taekwon-Do lesson took place on an indoor 100 metre running track. There was a definite fitness section to the lesson which involved laying down on our backs half way down the track, jumping up, running to one end, then running the length of the track, then running back to the middle (so 200 metres in total) then do repetitions of whatever exercise Steve had called out at the beginning. No one wanted to finish in last place either. It didn't take me long to realise that, despite being eighteen years old and working out regularly this was a hard and very different type of fitness. This fitness burned deeper in my muscles and made my lungs push hard against my chest. I hadn't struggled for breath like this in Karate.

It felt good.

The exercises must have gone on for an hour. I was the new guy and had taken my karate stuff to wear so that I looked the part. This didn't work because the Taekwon-Do *dobok* (uniform) is somewhat different to the Karate *Gi*. The dobok is a lighter material with a Velcro fastening strap in the centre at the front. My gi was a wraparound gi and heavier material. The dobok has a logo and writing on the back of the jacket and the letters ITF down the outside of each leg and my karate gi had no decoration at all but I wanted people to know I was a purple belt and therefore be afforded some respect. Looking back this isn't strictly true: I wore my belt and gi as a way to tell people that I knew some shit. I might be new to this style but I had knowledge. OK that's not strictly true either: it's more likely I was trying to convince myself that I knew some shit even though I knew deep down that I probably didn't know half as much as I needed to know. I probably should have given myself a bit more credit. After all I had studied under Sensei and did exactly what was required and asked of me. You'll hear another saying that is often quoted in martial arts: *there's no such thing as a bad student. Only a bad instructor.* Sensei wasn't a *bad* instructor but in my 23 years of experience I certainly believe that his class needed a lot more realism and free flowing scenarios.

In my mind I was trying to convince myself that because I had done some gradings I had earned respect. It's worth mentioning here that there is no purple belt in Taekwon-Do so the Taekwon-Do students didn't have a clue what it represented anyway.

So I went all in with the exercises to make sure I didn't get left behind. After all it would never do to be beaten by people who hadn't graded as much as me (not that I knew what each colour belt meant anyway. Apart from black belt). How I made it through that part of the lesson I will never know. I don't know whether it was the exercises themselves or me trying to hide my exhaustion that I found harder. After that section we were afforded a well-earned yet rather short break to rehydrate and catch our breath. In my case also inhaled a fair bit from my asthma inhaler. I was born with asthma, which sucks (no pun intended), but I've always worked through it.

Towards the end of the lesson the guys did some sparring. This fascinated me. I hadn't seen people fight before like this and it looked fun. I paid attention to the equipment that they used- the gum shields, the sparring gloves and foot pads, groin guards and sometimes shin pads. I figured there was a degree of risk with sparring if these guys felt the need for this level of safety equipment and I liked it. Steve had asked me if I had sparred before and I had said no so he said I could just watch for the moment. That was fine with me for now. I was curious but still didn't want people to think I couldn't fight. I didn't want to lose face like I had done in my high school.

I watched these people pit their wits against opponents of similar size or grade. They had expressions of intense concentration on their faces as they looked for openings and ways to attack. Every now and then they might make little 'faking' movements to lull their opponent into blocking or trick them into creating an opening and then- WHAM! Explode into a kick squeezing their foot through a tiny gap in their opponents defence. The safety pads that they wore would often make loud, clapping sounds on impact which added to the impressive and explosive nature of the fight.

I thought they looked a lot looser and more fluid than the karate guys that I had trained with too. A lot of what I was used to was strong, straight movements. I had trained with weights to get as strong as possible in the belief that the stronger I was the easier it would be for me to defeat an attacker. Karate would cement this strength into a coherent syllabus to make it useful. Although strength is an advantage I had not found it to benefit me in any way as yet because I had not tested it.

I was about to get that chance.

After a few rounds, Steve asked me if I would like to give sparring a go. I was incredibly keen after my observations, naively thinking that I had analysed this style enough to fight and having enough confidence to believe that I could 'show these guys a thing or two'. In hindsight I am not sure where this bravado came from (I had not done any previous sparring, remember) but I badly wanted to be included in this part of the lesson. I borrowed some gloves and pads from others in the class.

The chap that Steve had chosen for me was a tall, lean guy who was a keen boxer as well as a martial artist. The Boxer was approaching black belt and had been training consistently for some time. He was probably six foot three and easily taller than me with a long reach. He had a typical boxer's build- lean and strong. He also wore a slight smile on his face and looked very calm and laid back about what he was doing. I did not mistake this laid back appearance for ignorance but that he looked at ease with his ability. Relaxed if you will. I believe I would have been his opposite in this regard. If he was the wise old dog quietly summing up the scenario to work out the best possible path to success I would have been the young, hyperactive puppy jumping around like a mad thing keen to get on with it but with absolutely no method at all. I knew that the low and set stances of karate were not applicable in this arena but was sure that my karate grade was about to be consolidated and that the 'enlightening knowledge' that my Sensei had passed on would magically start to work just like it did for *Daniel- San* after he had washed Mr. Miyagi's car and painted his house and stuff.

I believe that the round lasted two minutes. There were several breaks as The Boxer scored easy points with fast and fluid techniques. I was not afraid to do my thing. I could throw a kick and punch and happily attacked as often as I could. I was not shy of attacking. In short I wore myself out quite quickly and had to rely on pure youth and energy to get me through. My ignorance of sparring was, in this case, one of my advantages because I had no fear of getting hurt. It also wasn't a real encounter so confrontation wasn't an issue either. Those emotions that I wanted to confront were pushed to the side in favour of excitement and fun. This was fighting but in a class environment. The teacher and student atmosphere expelled any malice in attack and the pads that we wore went a large way to reducing injury. There were also rules to this fight like no holding, no attacks below the waist and a referee. Although I was able to let go of my fears and just see what my techniques could do I did not use them in as realistic a way as I might have done in a real attack.

I was able to relax a little bit knowing that I was not the victim of bullying or a malicious fight and enjoy it. Techniques came from my arms and legs and, although often misguided and misplaced, I believe this was a positive martial experience for me. I did get a few techniques through just by sheer volume but these were far outweighed by the polished and accurate style that my opponent possessed. If The Boxer hit me it affected me psychologically and made me want to hit The Boxer back even more. I was told which targets would score points in a competition. Every time The Boxer hit me he scored a point. I needed to get a point back quickly to even the score up. If anything I went in too quickly after receiving a punch or kick without enough thought and strategy. It was nice to have a feeling of wanting to get stuck in though.

At the time I was unaware that a crucial part of the martial arts was missing for me. *Pressure testing* is important in anything. If you want to know if you are getting better at something there is no better way that putting yourself slap bang in the middle of a situation where you have to use it (within reason). I realised in time that I would have to go about my training with a slightly different approach but for now I had found a method of progressing from kata and set movements to something more 'real' and less rehearsed. Something that I could interpret and develop as my own.

From that first lesson I was hooked on Taekwon-Do and this is a style that I still practice to this day. That style allowed me to open up and be myself whilst training. I felt that I could apply what I was teaching and didn't follow Steve blindly but rather in a consultative manner where he would not just show us moves but how to apply them and in which scenario that technique would be most suited. It would be fair to say that Steve has played a larger part in me staying with that class than the style itself. Steve, if you are reading this one day: thank you. Thanks for the years of tuition, persistence, patience, advice, mentoring and friendship. You are exactly what it means to be a martial artist.

Since the days when I was eighteen years old I have seen innumerable kids come through Steve's class and grow in character and self-confidence in the right way. This is an indication of how I was taught and I teach so that this knowledge can now be passed on with confidence to future generations to use to better themselves.

I have mentioned the psychological impact that martial arts can have on the student. One of the characteristics that should improve is self-confidence. I am not saying that everyone who takes up the martial path has had a mentally disturbing experience or has been bullied for years but let us not forget that martial arts are combat systems designed for war or combat and therefore self-protection. Confidence in oneself is an integral part in holding your own and being able to develop in your style. A beginner should not be too quick to display their confidence but rather take their time to settle into training. Over the years I have seen many students come and go and yet only a small number of these remain. Lots of them expected too much too soon and didn't have the will power to persist in their efforts. Shame really as lots of them had some decent talent. As mentioned before there is a type of practitioner who stays to get what they think is a master level and then leaves believing that they are the mecca of all things martial. These people have mistaken self-confidence for arrogance.

Self-confidence should grow at an even and relatively slow pace. Over the course of going from white to black belt the student will have peaks and troughs in their self-confidence and believe in their ability. They will beat opponents whom they though would not be penetrable and lose to others whom they outrank in belt and experience.

Never under estimate an opponent. Remain humble to learning. Remember that as long as you train you can control your own self-confidence, personality and exercise regime but cannot necessarily change natural talent. Apart from the elite few, there will always be someone better than you and you will always be better than someone. It is healthy to find perspective in your ability and set realistic goals and aims for your training.

Over the years I have been elated and disappointed by many fights both in the arena and real life. I have been disappointed with how I have won fights and delighted with lessons learned from some losses. It is important to realise your purpose for training and remain calm and level headed when the outcome of your endeavours are not quite as you expect. There will be a reason for it and when you find the reason you will find a way to overcome any challenge. The journey from white belt is an amazing journey and I remember being a white belt and having a thousand questions built up by the time I had taken my first grading. You find the answers come naturally as you progress through the ranks and travel from the last line in the hall to the first line in front of the instructor. You will find that a decent class will yield senior grades and instructors who never tire of answering your questions and queries. They will know answers or be able to point you in the right direction. You should have confidence in them. If you do not, you may need to question whether that class, style or instructor is the right one for you. I don't think it is unreasonable for someone with an interest in studying martial arts to go to several different styles and do a 'taster lesson'. I have mentioned previously that you may need to ask yourself a few questions about what you want to learn:

- If you want to kick and punch you might choose Taekwon-Do, Muay Thai or kick boxing.
- You may want to be able to fight from the ground and choose Brazilian jiu-jitsu or Sambo wrestling.
- You may want more of a traditional self-defence aspect and choose Japanese Jiu Jitsu or Aikido.
- You might want to throw an opponent and study judo
- You might want to combine all these ranges and find a good MMA school (Make sure you can do a beginner's course or be able to learn at your own pace. MMA can be a bit over whelming).

This is what I was talking about earlier on in this chapter- which style is right for you. I mean, once you have decided that karate is for you (because there is no way Mr Miyagi was getting beat), which one do you choose form there? Shotokan? Shuko Kai? Shito Ryu? Kyokushin Kai? Goju Kai? Wado Ryu?
Who knew?!
What is the difference?

Does it matter?

Don't worry about it.

Firstly you may not have all of these styles locally to where you live anyway.

Secondly as long as you can research the name of the style a little bit and find a governing body and some stability you are likely to find a proper martial art rather than an off shoot.

Thirdly, how does the class 'feel' to you? Be honest about this. Don't naively follow 'Blind Master Po' just because he has a 15th dan black belt and can knock people out with his stare. Here's an example:

After many years of training in Taekwon-Do I decided that I needed to improve my arsenal in the close quarter's range of grappling and throwing. I found a local Japanese Jiu Jitsu class as I knew this style would likely provide the techniques that I was looking for. I held a black belt in Taekwon-Do at this time and decided not to mention this too quickly. It wasn't relevant anyway as Taekwon-Do did not overlap in technique with Jiu Jitsu anyway. I wouldn't benefit in any way by imparting this knowledge and, in previous experience, may set myself up to be the example of why Jiu Jitsu was better than my style. There are many instructors out there who like to profess why their style is superior. This doesn't interest me because it is complete bullshit. Better to look to the stylist rather than the style for class and superiority.

Anyway, the first couple of lessons were okay. The class covered many aspects of techniques that were really alien to me: throwing, falling, joint locking and manipulation and defence against weapons like knives, bats and swords (note: if someone actually does attack you with a sword, forget whatever training you think you know and get the fuck out of there). I didn't build up as much of a sweat as Taekwon-Do training but technically the instructor seemed to know his stuff and the techniques seemed to work once applied correctly.

Something didn't feel quite right though.

Although I found the training fun, the techniques were quite specific in their application. If applied correctly they could do damage to an opponent quite quickly but I believed that they had a high chance of going wrong and not performing their task correctly. Too many fine motor skills increased the chance of human error. One might argue that I didn't give this class enough time (I trained there for about 4 months) but I say otherwise. At this time I had 16 years' experience in martial arts having touched base on Karate, Taekwon-Do, Thai boxing, boxing and some Jiu Jitsu and MMA.

The final straw for my nagging doubts came when we were given a slot at the end of a class to do *randori* or free sparring. I had been waiting for this moment for some time. For weeks now we had practiced really cool looking throws and locks that would gain you maximum street cred in a real fight and I wanted to see how these guys held up in a 'free for all' way of sparring. I was disappointed to say the least.

I sparred with several of the students of varying ranges. The rules of this game were no striking at all. Win was by clear throw or submission. I found a lot of the guys would lean on their size and strength if possible regardless of grade. Indeed a strong opponent has a distinct advantage but the application of the techniques which they had been showing me was severely lacking. I even managed to throw a couple of them and the odd submission found its way onto my opponents too. I don't believe I should have been able to do this. They were not going easy on me. I know that so they should have dominated me and talked me through potential errors or opportunities.

It might have been fate that decided that, due to there being an odd number of students on that particular lesson, I found myself up against the instructor but whatever caused it, I was delighted. I have never shied away from a martial challenge and now I had what I wanted: a chance to see just how good I was on the ground if I went in all guns blazing.

This particular instructor was a 1st degree black belt in his style of Jiu Jitsu. When he taught and demonstrated techniques he looked fluid and knowledgeable although on closer inspection (and after speaking with several other people who had stumbled upon his class on their martial travels) he did tend to play to his own strengths. You see, he was 19 stone in weight and I am not talking weight built on pure gym time here. I am sure there are plenty of decent fighters out there who aren't as svelte as your average UFC cage fighter but come on! Let's lead by example here!

As we 'rolled' or sparred it became evident that he could not apply his techniques on me. I was pretty strong as I've always been a friend of free weights and every time he went to apply a lock or submission I felt it and could fight against it. It didn't take long for him to state that anyone can fight against these techniques and that in a real fight you would struggle applying a lot of the techniques. He also stated that me using my muscles to fight against his techniques had made me out of breath too quickly and that would hinder me in a real fight.

Really?!

I can assure you readers that, at 14 stone and as fit as I have been I most certainly had a more favourable lung capacity and aerobic level than this overweight instructor had probably ever had.

After a quick mental dissection of what was probably one minute of sparring I also realised that there were innumerable times where I could have let fly with punches and elbows and even knees which would have destroyed him in a blink. These guys didn't practice strikes with their ground fighting. I had discovered another dimension which I needed to apply which this class did not yield.

I was bitterly disappointed. I should not have been able to hold my own so easily against this instructor. I felt like there was no point in staying there. I wanted an instructor who lead by example. I had been teaching Taekwon-Do for a while at that point and I know what example I lead by.

I finished that class and never returned. I am sure that they enjoy their training and a diligent student is bound to learn some useful techniques in any style of class but this was not for me. I had lost confidence in that instructor in the blink of an eye and no amount of verbal justification was going to make me understand why he couldn't apply his technique.

It is worth mentioning that shortly after leaving this class I found a decent MMA class and the instructor has a sound ability to apply relevant techniques to me and explain how he found a route to his victories and what I could do to improve my defence or attacks. He leads by example. Good lad! It certainly isn't the cheapest class out there but the quality of tuition coupled with the excellent teaching style of the instructor certainly makes it the best value through high quality technical information. It is also worth mentioning that my recent adventures into the world of Brazilian Jiu Jitsu (BJJ) are also very difference to my experience in their Japanese counterpart. When the Gracie's developed BJJ it was borne from Japanese Jiu Jitsu and Judo and greatly benefited the smaller man so my strength has been greatly negated. BJJ is the real deal. It just is.

So happy hunting. It may take you a while and you may have several disappointing experiences. You might find your ideal class on your first attempt. Either way just enjoy it and remember that if you leave a class out of breath, tired or with a few bruises you have probably had a good workout which is better than nothing.

Chapter Two
Taekwon-Do

You might get hurt; get knocked. You might feel afraid and not want to continue. That's fine. I get that. Just don't show it until the fight is over.

By the time I took my first Taekwon-Do grading I was happily settled into a routine of training. I was enjoying the fitness aspect of this style. Much of that ethos came from this particular instructor and I had a desire to push my physical limits to enhance my technique so I was well suited to this class and instructor.

Moving from white belt to yellow tag was not much of a transition for me. I had graded many times in Shotokan karate before now and was used to how it worked. Whereas Karate had their kata, Taekwon-Do had the same pre-arranged sets of movements but these were called *tul* instead. Taekwon-Do is Korean whereas Karate is Japanese hence the difference in words. The first sets of movements in Taekwon-Do were called four directional punch (*Saju Jirugi*) and four directional block (*Saju Makgi*). The first pattern was called *Chon Ji* and was very similar to the first kata- *Taikyoku Shodan* from Shotokan. I passed my first couple of gradings with ease and looked forward to a future filled with Taekwon-Do.

I think it is important to mention that whatever you are looking for in the martial arts must be weighed up by what time you are able to invest in it. At the current point in this book I would be 18 years old and at university undertaking a bachelor's degree in sports studies. I was plunged into a world where I was totally in control of my own time and could invest large chunks of my days to my training. This would continue for at least three years so my eagerness to learn was fulfilled by what I could invest. If training classes were on twice a week and the adult class followed the junior class I would not think twice about doing both classes back to back. This still did not satiate my thirst for knowledge so I decided to put a notice up on the notice board outside one of the university sports halls.

De Montfort University in Bedford was set on two grounds at opposing ends of the town. I lived in the halls of residence on Polhill Avenue in my first year directly opposite the sports hall.

It was ironic that there was actually a Taekwon-Do class already using that hall to train but I was already settled at my other class.

I wrote out a note on paper no bigger than a postcard simply saying that I was a student at the university and that I was looking for sparring partners and then put the phone number for my block where I was staying. It only took a week or so before I had a few replies and organised some extra training. I was delighted. If I am honest, this experiment was completely for my own benefit. I wanted to do more martial arts and maybe find someone who could assist in my learning by attracting senior grades to myself. I had a good result. Three people initially called me.

Paul came from a Chinese style background. He called this style *Tung Bay* and to this day I have not found anything to suggest what it is! It involved lots of circular movements though. Paul was a similar build to myself and extremely fit. He would soon join the same Taekwon-Do class as myself and remain there for his university days.

Then there was a guy who studied Shotokan karate. He was a black belt. I forget his name. He was a thoroughly nice chap and his karate class had obviously been more applied in their approach to the style than I had experienced. He had some decent knowledge of fighting and was keen to impart his wisdom on me to my benefit.

Then there was James. James was a 2nd degree black belt in ITF Taekwon-Do- my style of choice. James was around 15 stone of British beef and was not afraid to take a fight to his opponent. He favoured old school training and liked to involve some good, solid conditioning of the arms and legs through regular impact (conditioning is a form of strengthening limbs against injury through regular impact. It works. It hurts too. You might get injured. It's your choice.). James wouldn't think twice about suggesting that one of us stand still with our arms held out straight at shoulder height whilst the others took it in turns to kick them in the stomach. Suffice to say that I learned a lot from James.

We spent many hours just the two of us, at the student leisure centre, training, fighting, discussing and tweaking techniques. He outweighed me by several stone but taught me to play to my strengths and take the fight to an opponent through simple combinations of techniques that changed level. He was also the first person to tell me what is written in italics at the beginning of this chapter. This is about playing the psychological game of a fight. There's no shame in being beaten if you are experimenting and using new techniques or theories. The only way to prove or disprove a technique is to practice it. Don't sit in a comfort bubble doing what you have always done and wondering why it doesn't work as people around you progress. A black belt is just a white belt who has never given up. In BJJ that black belt will have tapped out 10,000 times to achieve their skill level. There's no shame in that whatsoever.

So I was 18, studying sport and training every day- sometimes in lessons, sometimes alone and sometimes with the 'support group' that I had engineered myself.

Surround yourself with like-minded people.

It is important to ask yourself two questions:

1) What do you hope to achieve from your studies?
2) What time can you invest towards achieving it?

You might be limited through work, family, fitness level or a whole myriad of other life issues that need to be considered. When someone asks me now, 'Adam, how much training should I do each week?' I answer 'How much time have you got?'. Most people will say about an hour or two but will neglect telling you how many hours of television they watch each week or what time they get up on the weekend. If you want to practice your style for two hours a week and spend the rest of it testing the sofa in front of Jeremy Kyle working your way through multi packs of crisps then that's fine. Whatever floats your boat. But don't expect to progress much. There's this little saying that I like: *if you put shit in, you get shit out*. I would assume that, by reading this book, you have an interest in achieving a black belt or at least a certain level of aspiration and ambition. So be realistic with your planning. If you only have an hour or two per week to invest in lessons, can you borrow any time from another area of your life? Can you get up an hour earlier to work on your fitness? (I do). If you really can't miss finding out whether that young spotty scumbag is, indeed, the child's father or whether Jeremy Kyle will indeed prove that the lie detector says she slept with her father's mother's brother, can you work out whilst watching the TV? (I do). Can you train with any friends if classes aren't on that evening? (I do). I've even been known to smash out a hundred press ups whilst on a toilet break from time to time (I always wash my hands). Be realistic but be honest with yourself too. The journey to black belt isn't an easy one but is an immensely rewarding one and does involve a certain amount of persistence. If you do not train frequently enough there may come a point where you halt in your gradings and don't progress as your instructor won't think you are ready for it. Worse still, if you have chosen a bullshit class or style, your instructor *does* grade you and you will have a false sense of your ability like I did in my karate.

Having started my journey at the age of fifteen I am now thirty seven and have no problem admitting that I am still learning and always will be. I learn from seniors and juniors alike. It will take everyone different amounts of time to reach certain goals. So if your goal is to get your black belt, fair play to you. Ask yourself this: How long will it take you to get it? In Taekwon-Do, if you took all of your gradings on time with the minimum time allowed in between your belts you could reach black belt in three to four years. What do you think of that? Doesn't seem too long, does it?! In some places you can even guarantee your black belt in less time- sometimes as little as 12 months if you pay enough...

For me thirteen years was the time it took me to get to black belt. I do not consider this too long at all. If you consider that I reached purple belt in karate after about two years I would have been a black belt in Shotokan after about 4 years had I continued in that style and passed all of my grading exams. A black belt in what though? I would have completed my journey without having undertaken a single bout of sparring or actual combat. Had I then been attacked for real my enlightening journey to martial excellence would have left me floundering like a fish out of water.

False confidence.

That journey to become an all-out warrior would have left me vulnerable to injury or worse.

There was a chap I know who studied Taekwon-Do. He graded on time every time and successfully achieved his black belt after about three and a half years. That was his goal. He wanted his black belt and he got it. Well done. Part of the syllabus of Taekwon-Do is to break boards with hand and foot techniques. This is included to test the efficiency of your technique over power and also, I like to think, test your bottle too. Now some people will be built of naturally harder stuff than others but there will be some who, no matter how quickly they want to get their black belt, will not be able to prepare for this part of the grading. When you punch a board with a fist it is likely that you will soon bruise your knuckle, cut your skin or generally hurt your hand or wrist. This may happen time and time again. This type of conditioning works on flattening the knuckles and making your bones stronger by continually breaking them down through injury, then building them back up again.

Imagine the bones are like a sponge and the healing process fills in the holes in the sponge. This is what makes bones harder and gives the martial artist the ability to break more and more boards or hard surfaces in general.

Now I don't care what anyone says you cannot build up the same sort of conditioning in a couple of years compared to maybe 10 years. You also can't buy experience. It depends what you are expecting of yourself. Let me put it this way- when push comes to shove and you are attacked by a couple of young scrags out for your mobile phone and wallet, would you rather have Joe helping you out who got his black belt after three years of training twice a week or Bob who got his black belt after taking ten years to build knowledge ands experience and wear the injuries of battles gone by?

The black belt has become a symbol of the end of the journey and you can find a black belt in any class in any town in this country. There are so many styles and classes that a black belt has lost its exclusivity. It should represent an elite group of stylists who lead by example. There used to be a time where, when someone found out that you did martial arts, they would immediately ask 'Oh right. So are you a black belt then?'. I think recently, people would find out you were a black belt and say 'Oh right. So you're a black belt then….Erm... great.'

A lot of this is due to the deluge of shit martial arts that have been turfed out in the last twenty years via shit martial artists. You know what they say- *you can't put a shine on a shit no matter how hard you polish it.*

You could go to a lot of classes now and there would be a range of black belts from accomplished to mediocre. Of course, individual style and skill does vary but the range is often too great in my opinion. Black belt means you are no longer a novice. It means you should be able to hold your own against a single opponent fairly comfortably. There should be standards which all black belts are measured against (which is the grading syllabus) but, much like a driving test, would yield interesting results if everyone had to retake their exam. If we label a black belt an expert in self-defence would you trust them to use their skills to protect your life or that of a loved one? Would you trust them in the same way that you would trust your NHS surgeons to operate on you? What about the skills of police officers, fire fighters or paramedics? What about the nursery nurses who look after the most prized possession that you have: your children? That is why I left that Jiu Jitsu class.

If you are looking for a way out of being bullied or attacked, like I have said, be prepared to invest time in your martial pursuits. Getting that black belt around your waist does *not* mean you will achieve what you think you will achieve. You may not *feel* how you expect to feel. Don't be in a rush. Let it happen. Chase it with fervour and keenness but do not be over zealous and arrogant.

I delayed my first opportunity to take my black belt exam because, after 12 years, I did not feel that I was worthy of wearing a black belt yet. My compatriots thought I was crazy but they didn't have my past experiences and didn't have to wear the belt in front of the whole class, did they?! It took another year of training and studying for me to really feel that I could do my instructor and myself justice. Wearing a physical black belt is not the same as mentally wearing your black belt.

It was around 1997 when I had passed a few gradings that Steve mentioned about a competition that was coming up. The Welsh Nationals. It sounded important to me. I wasn't sure I was cut out for a national competition but Steve had other thoughts. He firmly believed it would be a good experience for me so I decided that if Steve thought I could do it then I would do it. I said I would compete and started about upping my training accordingly. I had been involved in martial arts for around three years now and I was young and fit so I guess there was no reason why I shouldn't do this tournament.

A lot of clubs seem to stay within their own training halls and don't compete as much as they should. Some McDojos (false training halls with instructors teaching inferior quality martial arts) profess to teaching deadly arts on one hand but won't compete because they say they might kill someone. Yeah right. Others will compete within their own association only which means that all the entry fees and trophies stay within that association. If you are the sort of martial artist who travels the path of competition you will quickly work out which classes these are because you will train with them and be rapidly disillusioned with the skill level to the point of feeling a bit sorry for them. Those students who are happy to stay within the safety of their own class will only ever spar and train with a minute selection of fellow students. They will understand their opponent better than a stranger and because of that they will spar according to the training mentality of their classmates. This is wholly unrealistic and will turn a potential strategic stylist into a short term stylist who is limited in skill and adaptability. If you compete within your own style but outside of your own class you will fight against people who you have never met before. Much like a personality you will find that some you like and some you don't. In some fights you will feel comfortable and in some you will feel outclassed. That's fine. At least you have to figure out how to fight someone new. After all you never know who you might come up against in life.

If you fight outside of your own class and against different styles then you are really pushing the boundaries. I used to compete in East Anglia open style tournaments which would attract classes from several counties who trained freestyle Karate, Taekwon-Do, kick boxing, Thai boxing and some other stand up styles that I didn't know.

Rules allowed kicks below the waist and leg sweeps which were alien to me and it was interesting fighting against people who learned different syllabi and were used to different rules. It showed me weaknesses that I never knew I had and could work on. This is an example of cross style competition within the stand-up arena. If you really want to push the boundaries you would work towards doing an MMA or combat Jiu Jitsu fight but I would recommend that to be down the line of training a bit. Get some general experience under your belt. You want your first competitive experience to be a positive one and not one where you get smashed because you weren't ready.

Anyway, back to my story: Welsh Nationals. Extra training.

I was doing some more fitness work now and also working on getting some of my kicking techniques looking really good for the patterns section of the competition. It was normal for Steve to enter all of his competitors into all categories: patterns, sparring and destruction (board breaking) if relevant. Steve wouldn't really let you get away with just sparring or just patterns. He believes in a stylist being well rounded in their art and making the most of the experience.

I was happy with my progress and couldn't believe that I would soon be travelling to Wales and competing for my town in a national tournament. I thought back to years earlier when the norm was getting up and wondering what abuse I would endure at school and the nagging fears of confrontation and fighting that plagued me daily. Yet here I was, an adult, fit and healthy and off to try and be the best in my class and bring a trophy home for the club and me. Just the feeling of being involved in the build-up to this event kept me from sleeping at night. Although I was apprehensive I did not have the experience of competition yet. I had sparred with my fellow class students and I was still getting used to their fighting methods (as well as still trying to get the better of James in my extra-curricular training sessions too.) This naivety actually helped me somewhat because I did not have to deal with the adrenaline overload that comes after you have taken a massive beating. It was still a controlled tournament with a referee and there was no danger of being bullied. I was pressure testing my skill to the best of what options were available to me at that time but it is still true to say it could have been more realistic.

A week before the tournament I went to a normal Thursday evening training session held at one of the local school halls in town. After biking three miles from my campus to the hall I locked my bike up, went into the changing rooms, got changed and went into the hall where the guys were waiting for the class to start.

It was customary in those days to play basketball to warm up. It was fun and something a bit more interesting than static exercises. The kids liked it too. What was really cool was that this particular school catered for children up to the age of thirteen who were not generally too tall. To try and negate this the basketball rings had only been put up at nine feet- a clear foot lower than regulation height. In my last year at school I had enjoyed basketball and for me and a few of the other adults it gave us license to pull ridiculous moves out of the bag. Slam dunks and reverse dunks were the norm of those days and the juniors revered us as the basketball Gods that we were. They probably wondered why the NBA hadn't sent a scout along to our class and signed us all up. We never explained to them why we were so good. Would you?

As we dribbled and bounced our way into a decent game the ball came my way. I was situated out to the right of the ring just outside the three point line. As I caught the ball I thought I had enough speed to make a dash for it, take the cheeky two pointer and run to the other end to defend. I bounced the ball and started to run. I didn't get passed one step.

As I put my right leg out in front and put my weight on it something did not connect from my brain to my ankle and all stability left me. My foot twisted so that the bottom of my right foot now faced my left leg. Pain flashed from my ankle up the outside of my leg. The ball carried on towards the ring while I crashed into a heap on the floor crying out in pain. I held my leg in my hands and looked at my ankle which was already swelling so fast I swear it was visible to the naked eye. A couple of the guys helped me to the washroom where I put my foot in the sink and ran cold water over it. I needed to try and reduce the swelling and it was the closest thing we had to an ice pack. The pain was excruciating and to top it off I had had a massive adrenaline rush which had turned my good leg to jelly. Balance was a struggle to say the least.

The water didn't work. I was now the proud owner of a purple golf ball on the side of my ankle and Steve immediately took me to hospital whilst one of the senior grades took the lesson.

I must have waited a good couple of hours to see someone at the hospital but Steve wouldn't leave me. He stayed as long as he could and even after that evening he drove me home and fetched my bike for me too. It turned out I had torn a ligament in my right ankle away from the bone. It was bad. The Nationals were now a distant memory. I wouldn't even be able to spectate let alone compete. I was devastated and broke down in my room at the student block.

It is fair to say that setbacks will happen throughout everyone's lives. Sooner or later the proverbial spanner will worm its way right into your workings and lodge itself there, forever refusing to move. This injury took me about nine months to get over and along the way, might I add, some most amazing and vibrant autumn colours appearing in my foot from bruising and blood pooling. After a couple of months I was able to stand upright without a searing pain shooting down to my foot. After three months I was able to put enough weight on my foot to tentatively walk on tip toe again with crutches. After five months I was still in pain and had a swollen ankle but was so frustrated with not training I used to go to the sports hall and practice kicking standing on my good leg. The pain was intense. I didn't care. I needed to train so I worked through it. After about seven months I could ride a bike again and went back to training. After about nine months I was back to normal. Tough, painful times.

Whether it is an injury like mine, a work commitment, family commitment, pain in the backside ex, depression, addiction or something else, how you deal with it will be more important than its presence in your life. Sometimes you cannot help things happening. That's life. The strong minded person will expect setbacks and challenges and rather than let it get them down will embrace it and find a way around it. If you have injured yourself, although it is frustrating, it happens and you should recover in a sensible fashion so that you live to fight another day. If work commitments are building up or you can't find the time to train, do something about it.

'What? Change jobs?' you exclaim, 'Adam have you lost the plot? I can't just change jobs to suit my training!'

OK suit yourself but if you are looking to throw yourself into this game then why not? If you dream of doing something or being a certain person, what exactly is stopping you making changes to become who you want to become? Some people move Heaven and Earth to reach their potential. When push comes to shove, a lot of the excuses that people put up as a reason why they haven't progressed in life as much as they wanted are actually a load of bullshit. Great big steamy piles of it. People can have a natural tendency to listen to the negative side of their brain which can readily provide excuses as to why they can't/ haven't/ shouldn't do something. This provides a safety net if you will. A reason to remain in the safety bubble of their life and not push themselves. If that is where you want to remain then good for you but don't go around whinging that you are unhappy and that life had dealt you a bad hand.

As people progress through their martial path towards excellence they should deal with setbacks maturely. Injury requires healing. Time constraints require time management.

Stress requires acknowledgement and in some cases action to resolve. You should create a winning mind by believing that you are on the path to reaching potential. Think positive. Most predicaments in life have a solution. Some are just harder to find. If for reasons beyond control you cannot train or are stuck at a particular point or technique, look for all the alternative options to you and work positively to resolve the matter rather than find all the excuses in the world to give up. Expect setbacks. Embrace them. Analyse them. Find a solution. This is about mind set and how you think and interpret information. I'll give you an example:

You are standing at one end of an alleyway. You need to get to the other end. Turning round is not an option. The alleyway is dark and foreboding. Not friendly at all. There are high brick walls either side of the alley with barbed wire running along the length of them at the top. The alleyway is blocked half way down by a solid brick wall and between you and this wall are two huge, unfriendly guard dogs. They are growling at you and salivating at the mouth. What do you do? How do you get to the other end of the alleyway?

Take a few moments to think about this scenario. It looks quite hopeless and not worth the risk but it is an example of a scenario that might not be all that it seems. It depends on how you look at it and likewise how you look at life in general. I'm sure you've heard of the old saying '*is the glass half empty or half full*'? If your glass is half full you are a natural optimist and if it is half empty you are a natural pessimist regardless of the fact that there would be the same amount in the glass. I will talk about visualisation soon in this book- a technique that I use to help make things happen.

I was asked the above question in a job interview once. I don't really know why. I was going for an office job in sales. The job spec never mentioned guard dogs in an alley on a dark night but it did give me the chance to display my naturally positive disposition. So I answered the question as follows:

I would tell the dogs to be quiet because they are mine. They are just annoyed because I haven't fed them yet and it is past their dinnertime. I would then step over the wall because it is only a couple of feet high and go home with my dogs for dinner.

No problems for me there. I have moved away from introversion and fear towards positivity and optimism. My martial journey had greatly contributed towards this shift in my personality for the better. It has taken me from a teenage child full of fear and naivety to a grown man with knowledge and confidence and an extrovert and positive nature that seems to drive my wife around the bend on a regular basis (I have a tendency to be a tad childish). Over the years I have learned to be able to put things into perspective. Things that once would play on my mind for days or weeks now seem unimportant in the big scheme of things. In my mind now I wonder why anyone would worry about such things. Putting myself back into my younger mind I am not surprised why I thought that way.

There have been times in my life when I have had close to nothing- no home, no money, few possessions, friends or self-confidence. Believe me it is true to say that when you have reached a point in your life when you believe you have nothing; when you can't really see a future for yourself and think that everyone around you would probably be better off without you and you have to drag yourself back up from the gutter you eventually realise that what you have in life is probably better than you think and, if you put (your current problem) into perspective, it probably shouldn't be causing you the stress and frustration that you are experiencing.

Eleanor Roosevelt said 'No one can make you feel inferior without your consent'. This can be transposed into any feeling so: 'no can make you feel stressed without your consent'. 'No one can make you feel frustrated without your consent'. 'No one can make you feel scared or frightened without your consent'. No one can form an impossible problem in their mind without their own consent.

Don't give consent.

Just say no.

It is just a question of remembering that you are in charge and as you progress through your studies you will learn more and more about combat, fitness and what you are capable of (physically and mentally). So look forward to overcoming those obstacles on the way because they will definitely happen and you will need to find a way to proceed to the next part of your journey.

Chapter Three
Competition

Visualise everything.
If you can imagine something happening then it will happen.
If you can't then it won't.
Either way you've made the decision and you are right.

Around the year of 1997/8 when I was in my second year at university I found a penchant for competition. In fact in a twelve month period our club went to fourteen separate tournaments around the UK. I went to all of them. After the disaster of the Welsh Nationals I took the time required to heal and get back to training and then I got stuck in. I took the next opportunity to compete without much persuasion as a testing ground, had a good experience and never looked back.

It is fair to say I had some success in my tournament career. I never returned from a tournament without a trophy or medal (or in some cases a certificate if the organisers were really fucking cheap). I base my success largely on my own attitude and efforts but also on the tuition of my instructor and the ethos of our club- that is very important to mention because I was given the correct level of encouragement by an expert in their field who knew what I was capable of better than I did at the time and had confidence in me.

That year was one of the most memorable and favourite years to date. The club was a close knit group of people all with common goals. I had some good friends training with me as a result of university 'networking' and getting to know the regulars too. I was making progress and feeling confident and more happy with life. There was always something to look forward to and I much preferred the competitions away from my home town of Bedford because it meant a whole day out involved in the art that I loved. It was also customary for our club to make sure we visited some sort of food establishment on the way back with the guys and kids who had come with which was cool. McDonalds was a favourite. Memories were built up through combat and socialising and the camaraderie kept us buzzing for hours after a tournament.

My first national tournament was the 1997 UKTA (United Kingdom Taekwon-Do Association) Nationals to be hosted at a leisure centre situated on the seafront at Brighton and gave me access to a powerful tool for my martial development.

It was a bright, cold and sunny morning and I was up early. Seeing this time of the morning was a rare occurrence in T Block in the university halls where I lived so I pretty much had the morning to myself. We had to be in Brighton by 10am to weigh in and register and it was a good two and a half hours away by bus so I was up at 6am to get ready. It was a great time of the morning to drink coffee outside whilst the air was still cool and fresh. The cold air revived my senses and helped me to prepare me for what lay ahead.

On this particular morning I was struggling a little and the coffee was a vain attempt to wake myself up. Steve and I had been at our local drinking hole, Princes Soul Café, until the early hours drinking Guinness, playing scrabble and generally debating the world and its contents. The Soul Café would always house a few regulars until early hours. I was discovering that there a few things that these regulars liked to do: invent random words whilst playing scrabble, drink Guinness and have crazy long debates about weird and random topics. All these things would happen at once so a single game of scrabble would probably take the whole evening. That place isn't there anymore. An unfortunate sign of the times I guess but certainly many happy memories of parties and socialising stay with me as well as some not so nice memories of a certain brand of over-proof rum but that's another story.

Steve was never too worried about us staying up late the night before a competition. This puzzled me somewhat. Maybe I assumed he took a traditional coaching stance on such events: 'make sure you have an early night before competing. No alcohol! No sex! You've got a long day ahead of you!'

Maybe I forgot that I was old enough to look after myself and that I had moved out of my parents' house some time ago. My upbringing was just fine but I wasn't exactly a responsible adult. Actually I can still be pretty irresponsible now but I have a wife so I just consider myself her biggest kid to look after along with our two year old and my twelve year old.

I did ask Steve once about preparation for tournaments and our late night sessions and he mentioned that a tournament is just sparring or pattern work on a set day and that in certain respects you shouldn't treat it as any different to any other day. After all, anyone can get attacked at any time and this may well be when you are tired, ill, sick, sleeping or even drunk. In that way, staying up late made the experience more real for me. At the same time he clearly meant that we should maintain a modicum of fitness all year round of course.

Sometimes I would have to dig deep to finish rounds of sparring during tournaments and invariably I would doze off in the car or bus on the way to or from a tournament too

.

After my coffee and a light breakfast I showered and checked my kit bag for supplies and clothing. I headed out through the university grounds to the front where I sat on a low wall by the roadside and waited to be picked up. After a short wait Steve turned up in a minibus with a couple of the guys and off we went.

I fell asleep in the bus.

On reaching Brighton it was clear to see that this was a decent sized tournament. There were lots of cars and coaches around the sports centre and I recognised some senior black belts and other people from our sister clubs and associations. The weather proved to be as positive as it could be too with a clear blue sky and sun shining down on us and spirits were high. We went inside and made our way to the main hall. I will never forget entering that hall and seeing several hundred Taekwon-Do students all warming up and practicing moves. The stands were full of spectators all waiting for the action to happen. Everyone generally mingled and chatted whilst kicking and stretching and checking equipment. The sports hall floor had been covered with blue and red mats which laid out 6 sparring areas for multiple categories to compete at once to save time. The whole spectacle of the event was really impressive.

After we had found a spot to put our stuff and warmed up for several minutes I heard a loud clapping sound. Everyone stopped what they were doing and turned to face the entrance to the hall. I was new to this type of event so I copied everyone in a round of applause that welcomed the premier person in the UK into the hall: Grandmaster Rhee Ki Ha 9th degree. I was honoured to be in the presence of the man who was responsible for promoting Taekwon-Do throughout the UK and as he addressed the hall my resolve to succeed strengthened.

The day laid itself out for everyone to enjoy and gave us the chance to show our worth at sparring, patterns and board breaking. I had brought some food for lunch but by the end of the day I was ravenous and very tired. Physical fatigue had been joined by mental fatigue and they were ganging up on me.

We left the hall at around 5pm and started on our journey home. I had ended up on a seat half way down the bus and my head was leaning on the window, bobbing up and down with the bumps of the road as I replayed everything that had happened that day whilst in a half sleep. I was happy not to socialise and chat. I was too tired and had too much going round in my mind. In my hand was a trophy. It was made of a piece of grey slate mounted on another piece so that it would stand up on a shelf of it's own accord. It was heavy and felt solid and had a figure sculpted on the front of it of a man performing a jumping splits kick and the words of the 1997 UKTA Championships emblazoned across it in silver. I had placed second that day for sparring. A good result.

My mind was active with thought and analysis and I kept going over and over the sparring that I had done that day. Had I earned this trophy? Could I have taken the gold? Questions arrived quickly and effortlessly and I was having to consciously slow down so I could answer them all.

After much though I was not concerned with taking the silver instead of the gold trophy. It was my first tournament and I had learned a lot about not just fighting but the preparation of the event and dealing with the excitement and adrenaline of the day. I spent a long time working out what had worked well for me and what I thought could have worked better. I was so involved in my post fight analysis that I didn't realise when we had arrived at McDonalds or, indeed, home later on.

The post-fight analysis is something that I still use today. Professional martial artists will also do this using video footage of their fights so that they can isolate areas to develop technique or application and put together a training plan accordingly. There is much to be learned from losing a fight. Sometimes more than you can learn from winning. Missing out on that winning decision means that there is definite room for improvement and therefore you need to search for a reason why you didn't win and work on them in subsequent training. Winning a fight is more objective in that you have already found a method to succeed and now need to find a route to hone that skill or achieve the desired result in less time or expend less effort. No one will ever win every fight so lessons can most certainly be learned whether you win or lose. As long as you are trying to better yourself and putting in your best effort then that is what counts and you are sure to move towards your potential. So post fight analysis is the practice of reviewing a fight that you have already undertaken and evaluating it for improvement and future success. *Visualisation* is a method of developing mental imagery to improve a desired outcome. In the case above, it would be to imagine how my fights would have turned out before I had actually participated. Visualising how you want a fight to play out can be termed as a technique called *fast forward.* This is literally placing yourself and your opponent in your mind and imagining what will happen in as much detail as you can. Over the years I have developed my own way of undertaking this thought process and I can become very involved in it once I start it by playing out several different scenarios so that I am prepared for whatever might happen. Visualisation can help the practitioner to bolster their mental fortitude before confrontation. Some people are naturally brave and confident whilst the rest of us can use these types of methods to bring our mental state up to speed with our physical ability. Being able to imagine all the techniques of a fight, like watching a film, is a powerful tool to help your mind get to grips with the reality of what might be about to unfold. I have, on many occasions, visualised an upcoming confrontation with so much detail that my heart has started pounding at key points. My adrenaline has rushed through me at the moment before combat. I have even felt the elation and relief after the fight and sometimes even where I believe I might get injured and have to push through a pain barrier. I have used visualisation before regular training routines to improve my motivation to try hard and have a good training session and found myself actually starting to sweat whilst running through exercises in my mind. I would highly recommend researching visualisation techniques and work on using it to your advantage. It is certainly not limited to martial arts. I use visualisation for my day job in advertising, for my parenting skills as my daughters grow up and in other life aspects to try to better myself through adequate preparation.

I started training in mixed martial arts around 2010. I talk about how I started this project later on in this book but suffice to say that I was on a 'sabbatical' from Taekwon-Do to stretch my boundaries a little further than Taekwon-Do allows. For those of you that don't know, mixed martial arts (or MMA) endeavours to combine effective techniques from all ranges of combat into a hybrid style, highly individualised from fighter to fighter and tested in rings and cages in spectator events accordingly. Whereas traditional martial arts tournaments can happen at any given time and competitors can compete in several rounds and a variety of disciplines in one day, MMA bouts tend to be single bouts and the fighters will train for many weeks for a single fight of up to five rounds of five minutes.

Having spent several month learning techniques in alien ranges (and several more months recuperating from bruises and injury) I was in a position where I would shortly look for my first match up. Although it was just a consideration at this stage (I hadn't talked to my coach about anything yet) I had started a visualisation process to see how I thought an MMA event might play out for me. I didn't know where it would happen so I used a local venue which had previously hosted some fight events where I had spectated so I knew the layout and atmosphere. I chose for this event to happen during an evening rather than daytime. I tried to 'design' an opponent in as much detail as possible down to the expressions on his face, hair colour, build etc. I visualised what I would wear, having my hands wrapped and the all-important walk out to the cage to various favourite tunes of mine.

In my mind, I won that first MMA fight a thousand times over. I broke into the sweat of combat without even leaving my chair and performed my walk to the cage, entrance to many different music tracks and the full fight laid out in several different scenarios in slow motion, to music like in a movie and even with pausing on certain scenarios like in the Matrix! I visualised my changing of emotions throughout the whole event. Smelt the smell of the hall and spectators. Heard all the sounds that I might hear.

I concentrated on choosing techniques that I will win that fight with to attempt to 'programme' certain techniques into my mind for when they are required

Sound realistic?

Maybe not to you but to me visualising the event in this much detail is one of my most treasured possessions in my training camp. Bear in mind that I now teach classes and so I don't have time or finances to afford an amazing training camp with other instructors, unlimited time and amazing nutrition. I am a middle aged man with a family and two jobs so I will take any technique that I can to use to my advantage.

I can visualise the fight and experience the emotions and then fast forward to how I will feel when my victory hand is held up too. I condition myself to expect what may happen and thereby bolster my confidence and optimism in the right direction to help perform at my best. Visualisation helps me to believe in myself and be victorious.

I also use visualisation to imagine pre-fight training too. Think of those scenes in the Rocky films where Stallone suddenly gets his head down and cracks on with some hard training and you're shown scenes of exercises, drills and sprints to music. Nike did a series of adverts which exemplifies this type of motivational message a while ago where athletes would be faced with physical and mental hardship and have to dig deep to overcome these obstacles through hard training. They are worth watching. You can see these by going to YouTube and searching for 'Nike Motivational Commercial'. (It's also interesting to note that Nike rarely even mentioned their own products. They sold through emotion; shows how powerful emotions can be). I can envisage the weeks or months of training before hand, going through blood, sweat and tears to improve my technique and fitness. I can imagine actually getting fitter and feeling stronger and more athletic and therefore feeling more competent. When I run through these scenarios I can realise that the only thing separating me from this ideal being in my scenarios is performing a series of exercises in a sensible sequence over a set period of time whilst consuming good quality nutrition.

It puts into perspective what time and effort will be needed for me to properly train so that when I step into that arena I will fight knowing that I have put in every ounce of effort leading up to the fight that I could and therefore the outcome is a product of the 'best of my ability'. If I am truly fighting to the best of my ability then in my mind I have already won the fight. I mean what could feel better than knowing that you really did your best? That is something to aspire to. There is a distinct psychological advantage to thinking this way before the fight. At the beginning of this chapter it said:

Visualise everything.
If you can imagine something happening then it will happen.
If you can't then it won't.
Either way you've made the decision and you are right.

If you then consider what would happen if you consistently visualised getting your head kicked in, easily, in front of hundreds of people and feeling completely embarrassed, humiliated and worthless then you are unlikely to be in a great frame of mind come fight day. But this is what people often do! They will come up with all the reasons why they won't win or succeed. Have you ever challenged someone to something and they come out with 'OK but I won't win because....' Or 'OK but I've never done this so don't expect much....' The mind-set has already been explained to you and that person has built a mental fortress around their self-esteem to prevent it from being demolished or broken down. When that person undertakes that challenge or task and doesn't succeed or win, they invariably wear a sarcastic expression of surprise on their face and wisely say, 'told you.' They knew they would fail. They told you so.

They were **prepared** to fail.

Why would you prepare to fail? To keep yourself in your safety bubble? Maybe if someone got challenged to an arm wrestle, they might be afraid to win in case other people started challenging them until they lost. Maybe a martial artist would settle for silver because they are happy enough with it and have gotten away with their fights without getting hurt so far and don't want to push their luck.

The ethos of the individual who throws themselves into a task whole-heartedly and tries their best is a person who is more likely to be successful in their endeavours.

I also *fast forward* to after I have won the fight and what I will feel like. I tap into positive emotions: self-worth,, elation, joy. The beauty of visualisation is there are no limits apart from the edges of your own imagination. I could fast forward to after a fight and being in the centre of a press interview where reporters are holding their microphones towards me and firing questions at me on how I managed to defeat (opponent) and where did that amazing knock out technique come from? I can imagine running through my answers in great detail like a 'post fight analysis' and educate myself and the crowd on the finer points of the fight. I can visualise sitting in my lounge later that evening and running through words that might be appropriate for me: success, ambition, accomplishment, progression, ambassador to represent my club, aspiration, role model. (In the above scenario it might also be true to say that I've fast forwarded myself all the way into the UFC whilst rewinding my age and won't be happening in this lifetime because it's taken me too bloody long to grow up and learn this shit.)

The world is your oyster. In your own mind you can catch a glimpse of yourself at the peak of your own potential and performed in the right way, you can help carry yourself towards where you want to be.

I can just see you lot now, giving visualisation a try and ending up a billionaire with a Ferrari and perfect looking partner, six pack, all smiley white teeth and Rolex watches, basking on a white, sandy beach on your private island in the sun with a fucking butler bringing you cocktails. Whatever floats your boat I suppose.

There is another technique whereby one can literally pick a role model and attempt to emulate them- their behaviours, how they carry themselves, their style etc. Imagine trying to emulate Bruce Lee: the ability to successfully adopt his style of fluidity and confidence would be a distinct advantage in the fighting arena. You would become a 'martial chameleon'.

Please understand I am not suggesting you live your life in a false fantasy world where you are an invincible ninja assassin whose sole purpose is to go around destroying impossible adversaries. Leave that to Marvel. These are recognised techniques of cognitive control and should be used in context. Make sure you keep your visions realistic and achievable (if you have imagined yourself as the world's first white belt world champion, give yourself a slap and go back to page one of this book). Above all, make sure your visions are **positive**. Just as you can positively influence your thoughts by visualisation, you can also negatively influence them by thinking in a defeatist way. Don't fall into that trap. Once on the downward spiral it is harder to pick yourself up. If you are thinking positively about a fight then even if you lose you will already be looking for developmental points from your post fight analysis to achieve a better outcome next time. You will live to fight another day mentally as well as physically.

It is also important to get the balance right with your training. There is a distinct difference in available time if you are a young, single person compared to a middle aged family man with a stressful job, four martial arts clubs to teach and children (me). Martial arts are not necessarily about enjoying a hobby a couple of times a week. It can become an addiction and easily consume the student to the point where their training is all they think about. Having said that martial arts all tend to promote 'balance' in life. So if you have other commitments then look carefully if you feel you are tending too heavily towards a certain aspect in your life.

When I was in the third year of university I worked in a cocktail bar in the town centre and worked my way up to assistant manager. It was a full time role and I lived above the pub in the huge living quarters spread over two floors. As you can imagine I was the envy of my friends with unlimited access to my own bar and food and only one flight of stairs to negotiate to carry on a party.

Good times.

During my working hours I got to know a French girl who had travelled to the town to work and learn English so that she could go and work on a cruise ship. She had come into the bar to have a coffee and we had got chatting from there. One thing led to another and before long she had basically moved in with me above the pub. I was over the moon. I had a good job and a lovely girlfriend who wanted to stay in the country to make a future with me and was happily studying for my degree in sport. I didn't have many lectures at that time so I had no problem finding balance. I wasn't training much but for a while I relaxed into my work and love life.

Once the first semester finished at university that year the second semester brought a deluge of lectures and with it more work as the festive season approached. I found I could not find balance anymore and something had to give. Naturally as a student it was the job. I was in the second semester of my third year at university so it would have been crazy to quit my studies. I was working up to 80 hours per week and studying was nigh on impossible. Training was non-existent.

My girlfriend and I moved out of the pub and into a little one bed flat across town and I spent time on my studies. I went back to training too as I had bags of free time to use up whilst my girlfriend was at work.

Steve had recently taken over a building to try and give the club some stability in their training. The hall was situated near the town centre above a charity aid warehouse. I loved it. It had thin green carpet that tore your feet up after hours of training and bare bricks on the wall. A huge hole sat at the top of the wall at the far end of the hall where some kind of vent or air conditioning unit might have once sat and opened up the hall to the elements. We certainly trained hard that winter to make sure we stayed warm! The raw layout of the hall meant there was a huge reinforced steel joint running its length just above head height and Steve had hung two punch bags up- a luxury we had not had before. we also had a stereo for our cassettes (Google it) and CDs and even some prehistoric weight training equipment. All in all it was spit and sawdust and, in my opinion, perfect.

At that time work was also keeping Steve busy. For a little while now there had only been a select few of us training and so to keep the flow Steve gave me a key to the hall and said I could use it whenever I wanted (oh, go on then...). I don't honestly think I could have been happier. I was really back into my training and now had unlimited access to facilities day or night. If Steve wasn't around he would call me ask if I could open up the hall for regular training times which was fine.

A lot of the time there were only a few people there. Sometimes just me. But the class had to be open. It was my duty to make sure Steve's facilities were available for anyone who paid their dues and might want to train.

What I did not count on, though, was that whereas I was training at two or three of the classes a week in months previous and doing personal training at other times I was now opening the class up at every session and also using the hall for my own training. I had lost balance and it wasn't long before my now fiancée had had enough. I was given an ultimatum to cut back on training or else she would leave. I was pretty upset because through selfishness I had gotten used to this way of living where I was training when I wanted. I had taken my fiancée and my lifestyle for granted and now I had to change to retain the balance.

Unfortunately it was too late and soon after my fiancée left England to pursue her career aboard a cruise ship. She ended up travelling the world on the cruise ships and, after a spell in Miami and a failed relationship; she is settled in Portugal with her own sea front salon and a small dog. She's happy and we sometimes chat on Facebook. I'm pleased for her. I wouldn't say she has found balance in her life; not completely anyway. But she is always smiling in her pictures!

I'm not saying you should always cut back on your training if you have a family. Hell it's your life do what you want with it- train every night if you want. All I'm saying is make sure your family and friends know from the start what your intentions are and if you intend to shift your life balance somewhat to favour martial arts do not expect everyone else to understand. Just don't. Friendships may change along the way and it is your choice to decide how important they are to you. in my opinion, your true friends will always be there regardless. Family might take a bit more consideration.

Chapter Four
Weights and waits

It doesn't have to look pretty. It just has to work.

It has been 2 years and 6 months since writing my last words in this book. Sometimes that is just how life goes. Recent commitments with family, work and personal issues have kept me well away from the luxury of writing and placed my feet firmly on the ground of corporate development, parenting and teaching. I am what you might call typical Taurian (if you believe in that sort of crap) in that I do not openly welcome change. I have always been a creature of habit and enjoy finding routines to stick by and change as *I* choose. That being said, as I get older I am rapidly coming to understand that change is inevitable in life and for one to cling to a present constant is more a trait of keeping oneself inside a self-imposed safety bubble where nothing is unexpected and therefore nothing can threaten ones existence to any great degree.

This is, of course, unrealistic.

Nothing remains the same. And so rather than shying away from potential changes and curveballs in life it is often more productive and far less stressful to accept what may come and embrace the new challenges that change may bring. If life moves in the way that you want then you could substitute the word 'change' for 'evolution' and that puts a whole new perspective on what might happen. I mean, who doesn't want to evolve? To grow? To reach their potential and be the very best that they can be?

When my university education finished in 1999 I was back working at the cocktail bar. It was anything but ideal: working too many hours a week with no time to do anything for myself let alone train in Taekwon-Do. My girlfriend had left to travel the world on an exciting new adventure and to top it off my application to join the police had been turned down. I did try to get this decision over turned by appeal but that failed too. I had been unsuccessful on the ground of being "deemed unfit to be a police officer" (verbatim). I had passed the criteria for the fitness test but the decision was based on my having asthma and having obtained a reliever spray through prescription within the last twelve months.

"If I were to be chasing a criminal and have an asthma attack, what then?"
My immediate thought was turn around and go back to any number of currently serving fat police officers who gave up the chase long before me to see if they wanted a puff on my asthma spray but I didn't voice that thought. The only reason I had that spray on prescription was force of habit. I kept the spray next to my bed. I didn't use it but felt comfortable with it near me. The last one had passed its use by date. That was my safety bubble. I had put myself into it and kept myself there and now it had prevented me from being who I wanted to be.
My appeal was through letter to the Chief Constable of Hertfordshire Constabulary. It culminated with me offering to take on any officer in the county at the fitness test and if I beat them then surely I could be deemed fit to join?
No.
Well, in a more subtle way I received a letter that stated that it might be better for me to refrain from such challenges and wait the mandatory twelve months before reapplying as I might not be allowed to try again if I kept up with my letters. I can't deny I did exhibit a certain level of persistence that was unrivalled by most.

I had to wait twelve months.

This seemed like a lifetime and I remember reading that last letter from the force in my bedroom, alone and breaking down in tears as I realised that I had nothing in life that I had hoped for. No fiancée. No decent job. Plenty of debt. Living in a shitty little flat surrounded by memories of what I wanted but couldn't have.

Just a short while before my fiancée left to travel the globe I started working out with some cheap sand filled vinyl weights from Argos. I think I only had about fifty pounds of weight in total and just two dumbbells but I thought I would start throwing them around like I used to when I was living at home with my parents. I wasn't sure of what I wanted to achieve but I'm glad I found those weights. I remembered the positive feeling they had given me when I was younger. It's funny sometimes how a small, seemingly insignificant action or phrase could alter your path in life so significantly. Bruce Lee would liken this to dropping a pebble in calm water and watching the ripples eventually covering the whole of the surface.

I found a job in sales. This is what everyone does when they can't do their first choice of career. They sell stuff. I didn't really know what the job entailed apart from I would be wearing a suit and sitting in a large office with about 200 people selling what was the first type of digital TV set top box that was made (what a piece of shit that turned out to be). In hindsight it was a good time of life. The office always had a vibrant atmosphere, the people were all nice and I was actually pretty good at selling. This meant bonus which meant a bit of cash in my pocket.

The nature of the job was that we would receive incoming calls our headsets alerted us to an incoming call and we would try to sell a digital box to someone. On some shifts the headsets just didn't stop going off. On others time would pass slowly and there was plenty of time to chat with those around you. On one such shift I was talking about weight lifting and sport with someone and a young man sitting behind me overheard what we were talking about and joined in the conversation. I'll call him T. T was over 6 foot tall and incredibly thin. He wanted to know about weight lifting as he was quite self-conscious about his size. He owned some weights and a bench which he kept in his bedroom at his dad's place. After chatting for a while he asked if I might like to go over to his to train one evening. He really wanted someone to give him some direction in how to get big and he knew I had some knowledge from my degree and previous weight lifting. I was only too happy to find a training partner and a new friend so the timing was good for both of us. I accepted and we worked out.

As I become more involved in my weights I put my martial arts to the side for a while. It wasn't really a conscious decision. It was just that when I had the time to train I chose weights. This was a time when I didn't fight the change but rather accepted what was happened and relaxed into the flow of life. T and I trained several days a week and would dedicate each workout to one or two body parts. The type of training that we did was more appropriate for a bodybuilder with several years of training behind him than two rookie wannabees but we enjoyed ourselves.

Eventually we decided that in order to get the best out of our training we would rent a flat together for convenience. We found a nice place in a quite area of town. It was a clean, unfurnished two bedroom ground floor apartment and offered something more stylish and presentable than what we were expecting. We snapped it up and proceeded to find enough furniture from family and friends to be comfortable in our new surroundings.

T brought his weights from his dad's place but these had not been sufficient for some time. We gave in to progress and joined a local gym and had been working out there for a while. It gave us access to all the equipment that we needed as well as a swimming pool, sauna, steam room, tanning beds and a motivational place for us to be. We both needed to surround ourselves with positive influences in life and this was our home from home.

After several months of training we were making some gains but felt that we were not sure how to get to 'the next step'. We wanted muscle. We wanted big. I had wanted to have more understanding of the fitness industry anyway and so I signed up to take my fitness instructors award. (My degree was in sport but was quite philosophical in approach and so did not provide education in actual sports tuition or fitness). I booked a week off of work because the fitness course was in Basildon and I would need to get the train every day to get there. It was to be an arduous process but T and I both knew it would serve us both well in our quest for size. It also meant that I would be a qualified fitness instructor and might open up the avenue of going to work on a cruise ship. I was still hanging out for my French fiancée. I was young and stupid. Now I'm much older and much more stupider.

Most people at that time were signing up for the YMCA fitness instructor's award. The YMCA was the industry standard (and the one which you needed to work on a cruise ship too, which I didn't know at the time). I had gone with WABBA (World Amateur Body Building Association). To me it sounded more like the real deal and didn't include any of the girlie aerobics instructor awards that the YMCA insisted on dedicating time to (also needed for cruise ships). WABBA was the standard used by David Lloyds leisure centres and quite a few on my course worked at the David Lloyds where the course was held. I didn't like them. I had paid £200 to learn this valuable information and was dedicated to doing my best. There were others like me: dedicated to the cause and prepared to pay hard earned money for valuable information. The employees of the hosting leisure centre were fortunate enough to have their employer pay for their course and as such, did not value it as much. They already had their job and were intent on doing the minimum to pass and keep their job. They messed around and didn't pay attention. The class soon became split into two groups: those who were good, honest, seekers of the truth and the employee knob heads.

Day five of the course was exam day. I had booked myself into a cheap local hotel in Southend for the fourth night. One of the others was staying there and she gave me a lift to the hotel in the evening and back to the sports centre in the morning. I wanted to be well rested for my final examination. The hotel was an experience in itself.

It was winter and Southend was not exactly bustling with tourism. The hotel was playing host to some motorway maintenance men who were doing some local highway work. The atmosphere was none existent and the £25 room for the night was worth every penny but only just. It was run down and dirty. It reminded me of a room from a cheap horror movie where the bare light bulb would fail to illuminate the corners of the room leaving eerie shadows of doubt in each corner. If that light bulb gave up on me I was not sure whether I would see it through until morning. I laid down to sleep, listening to creaking floorboards and the footsteps of unknown men walking through the equally dank and dingy halls outside my door.

Morning came and with it the hope that I would see humanity again. I met my colleague downstairs for breakfast and then we set off for Basildon for our final day of testing. Suffice to say I did well and passed my course. I was handed my certificate along with the WABBA training manual and as much information as I needed for T and I to progress to the next level.

I spent that train ride back to Bedford reading that manual back to front and looking at how our programme would need changing. T was at the station when I got back to pick me up. "How was it mate? Do we need to change much?" He said. "T," I replied, "we're doing it all wrong....."

From there we abandoned our stupidly advanced routine in favour of a slightly more rounded strength workout which we hit three times a week with swimming and cardio days in between. We bought protein powder by the crate and aligned our work shifts so that we had the same free time. Things were good. Progress for me was good. T would have been happier making more gains but we are not all built the same and I did have a background of weight lifting from my teens that gave me a good start. I discovered that my WABBA certified qualification was useless without an aerobics qualification should I choose the cruise ship as a career but had no desire or money to sign up for an aerobics instructors course. I gave up on the hope of joining my ex fiancée on that cruise ship. It was inevitable anyway so it wasn't a difficult decision. In fact, once I had looked into the price of the aerobics instructor course and imagined myself and others dancing around in spandex and paying for the privilege I pretty much said "fuck it".
Besides, T and I were getting enough attention in the local clubs on a Saturday night to feed our egos anyway.
But as one door closes another one opens and a year had passed since my first application to the police had been turned down. I decided to try again and this time I was accepted having not needed an inhaler for over a year and not getting a prescription for one either. This meant more change. Change from my workout routine. Moving away from Bedford. Moving away from my friend and our flat.

Needing to learn to drive...

T had a car and taught me the basics of driving in a local car park and I bought lessons too, passing about 3 weeks before leaving Bedford for a thirteen week residential training course in Ryton-on-Dunsmore. Life was changing and so was I. I was about to make another friend who would have a massive impact on me in life.

Having passed my driving test I bought my first car six days before packing up my belongings and leaving Bedford. T and I are still mates today but this was the point that I started becoming more independent from him and our friendship took us on separate paths rather than the same one. My training course was thirteen weeks in length and from Monday to Friday. It was to be held at an old military base in the village of Ryton. This was one of the main training centres for the police. They had just expanded to provide some new residence to some of the fledgling officers. I was not fortunate enough to have one of these en suite rooms and instead had a box room with a hard, narrow bed and a desk. That was it. The carpet was rough enough to light a match on and each floor would share a bathroom and shower area.

Meals were provided too along with all uniform. Lessons and lectures would be from 9am until 5pm each day with a break for lunch and cigarettes as required. Most people smoked. I hadn't smoked in about fourteen months since working out seriously with T but it didn't take long for me to be a sheep and start again. Smoking would be a problem that plagued me for many years to come.

There was a large canteen where we would eat, a bar and lounge area where we would get drunk and a ramshackle gym which we could use as required. My eyes lit up when I saw the gym. The thought of going all week without working out horrified me as weight lifting had become my new norm.

When I say that the gym was ramshackle I am by no means under estimating the primitive nature of the room. The walls were whitewashed with few mirrors and the windows were dirty, single paned portals into a world of outside light. Plaster was peeling off of the white washed walls and if heating existed in the place it was certainly never on. The gym was a long thin room with some of the most basic and ancient machines you could ever see. Don't get me wrong; there was enough to do what needed to be done but you needed to strip the process back to basics in order to complete your workout. Machines were painted basic white and metal chains and handles were rusted and mottled. Seats and back rests were covered half in their original black plastic cover and half in silver Duct tape. (I now believe that no martial art or training place is complete without something being held together with Duct Tape. The stuff is awesome.)

Whereas the training area lacked luxury, the changing room did exactly the same. The ability of being an accomplished wordsmith and using fancy adjectives to describe this room are wasted here: it was a room with a shitty bench in it. That's it. A far cry from the luxury of the commercial gym that I was used to but had more of a feel of 'hard graft' that I sensed in martial arts halls than commercial gyms. It was familiar to me and I welcomed familiarity.

When the final yawns of the day were stifled at 4.55pm in the last lecture or seminar most would head to the canteen to eat and then get drunk in the bar. I would invariably head to the gym for a workout and then eat afterwards when the canteen was quiet. This meant that the gym would be quieter than normal which I preferred. There is nothing worse than waiting for the right bench or machine in a gym. My old commercial gym had been getting way too crowded for a while and I did not miss the queues for the flat bench one bit.

On one of my sessions I was one of two people in the gym. The other person was John. John lived to his own set of rules. He didn't follow the crowd if he didn't want to. He wasn't easily persuaded or coerced. John had an agenda. That agenda was to work out when he desired as he wanted to be fit and healthy. John was about the same age as me but thinner and was shifting some weights around to build up his strength base. We acknowledged each other but carried on with what we were doing. We had a workout to complete. Separately. But in the same room. But not together.

I think a moment must have come where we needed to use the same machine at the same time and, being the polite fellows that we were, decided to share the machine. We got talking from there and realised that we both had backgrounds in martial arts. Whereas my background was in Taekwon-Do his background was from Tang Soo Do. I could be really pedantic and split hairs about the similarities and differences of these arts but let's just say they were both stand up arts with kicking and punching.

John and I got on well. We started training together and a spark was lit within me for martial arts again as we used a dusty old pair of focus pads in the gym to practice kicking and punching. John had one of those nice, new en suite rooms which he revelled in (twat) and would often rag me about my less than luxurious living quarters (where the real men stayed). As time went on we would spend time in his room talking about martial arts and drinking whisky. We would use the lecture hall to watch old martial arts films (might I recommend that you seek out a parody of a Bruce Lee film called *A Fistful of Yen*- very entertaining if you know the film *Enter The Dragon*). We frequented a local country pub for steak dinners and generally struck up a friendship that is still very much valued to this day. I can firmly say that John will be a friend of mine for life and I consider him family and proud to say he is godfather to my youngest daughter.

Now I would like to take this opportunity to make something clear. This is my book and so I can write pretty much whatever I like so this gives me the opportunity that, should this book ever be published, I can immortalise my words in a way that is not matched through voice, text message or song. Even more so if I eventually self-publish. This is the written word. Documented for generations to come. For anyone who knows John and me and have read our text conversations or listened to us discuss martial enlightenment and combat history you will understand my next comment very well. So here goes: John, every time you think you submit me I am just tapping because I feel sorry for you.

During the sixteen months that I was in the police force I had been going back to Bedford on the weekend quite often as I missed my old town and life somewhat. It wasn't the same when I visited now though. I didn't live with T anymore as we had let the flat go when I joined the police. I didn't have a gym membership and was staying on the floor of a friend's house. It wasn't ideal but I felt the need to be back in Bedford. To be surrounded by that familiarity. After the thirteen week training course I had moved into a large four bedroom house in Watford which was where I worked. I had joined a local gym (where most of the criminals worked out) which was great but now that my martial fires has been lit I was finding myself going back to Bedford to train with my old Taekwon-Do instructor again. I would sometimes make the trip on a Thursday evening to do that session too. It was 47 miles from Watford to where I trained in Bedford but I needed to make the journey. The thought of not training was unbearable. John would sometimes join me for training. He lived around Stevenage at that time which was also where he worked and I would sometimes visit him instead of going to Bedford. John comes from a martial arts family and I felt privileged to train at his father's Tang Soo Do club. They welcomed me as if I were in their house as a guest.

I loved the police force but in reality I was young and didn't handle the grown up nature and responsibility that the force required. I believe I felt that my life was not settled in one place and I couldn't find peace of mind as a result. I was living with other officers who were not close friends. I was training at a gym without a set routine due to work shift patterns. My martial art training was infrequent and therefore didn't flow like it used to before. My life seemed like it was comprised of jigsaw pieces belonging to several different puzzles. The pieces did not fit together properly. My mind did not settle well with this disjointed lifestyle and something was about to blow.

An internal incident helped me to make the decision to hand in my notice from the police force and move back to Bedford. Something happened that made me realise that some of the people that I worked with were tossers so I thought "fuck this. I'm off". Please do not misinterpret that sentence for "all police officers are tossers" because they are not. I have respect for the police having done the job and walked the streets. I had an experience that was part due to me being immature in attitude and behaviour and part to do with those specific officers at that specific time in that specific station. It's not an interesting story I'm afraid. I was rubbish with administration and when I was off sick one day the sergeants needed some information relating to a crime that I was investigating. They opened my file and found themselves buried in paperwork. I had let it build up and it was my fault as well as being given too much to work on at the same time. My files were bagged up in an official evidence bag and tagged. On my return I was made to carry this through the whole station to the inspector's office to receive my bollocking which was demeaning and wasn't the right way to treat a young officer who was struggling. I accepted that I was wrong not to deal with my paperwork correctly and needed a kick up the arse but I still believe that the way that I was treated that day was akin to bullying and the biggest catalyst in me leaving the police force. I was about as lost as I could be really. I had no base to work from. The future was very uncertain, even looking at just a few days ahead.

I mentioned about embracing change a few pages back. Coming back to this point- the changes that were happening in my life were not as natural as life could dictate but rather induced changes instigated by me as I didn't really know what I wanted to achieve in life. When the opportunity to join the police force came up I took it as a progression in life. This experience turned out to be something different to what I had expected and so that progression was nullified and I was feeling that life was handing me one set back after another. I needed direction. I needed stability. I moved back to Bedford in the hope that familiar territory would provide me with inspiration to find out what I wanted to achieve with my life. For a while I lost contact with John. That was fine. Best get some peace and quiet from the old tosser for a while. I knew we would cross paths in our future anyway. From what I understand he got a bank loan for a car, buggered off to the Far East with it and hung out with some monks for a while.

Moving back to Bedford was good on one hand and bad on the other. At the time I didn't realise it but I was beginning to create this safety bubble again. Moving back to Bedford was, at that time, a regression in life rather than a bold step out of the box which I now advocate. I was returning to that which I knew best because the police force had placed a difficult challenge requiring hard work and effort on my shoulders and I wasn't ready or equipped in life to deal with it. Poor me. I took the easy option by moving back to Bedford. It involved a £10,000 pay drop too which would have most people recoiling in horror if it happened to them but I was so caught up in my own world that I didn't care. I wanted my old, carefree life back with my friends close to me.

I believe humans are predisposed to being lazy bastards and afraid to do things which aren't either guaranteed to work or take effort. A small minority will go against this and will challenge themselves on a regular basis. They will extend their boundaries of potential and stretch the limit of their mental and physical abilities and to hell with the consequences if they fall flat on their face trying; they would rather endure the painful graze of a face-plant than not to have tried in the first place. These people who are in constant search of their potential are, I believe, those people who become famous athletes, singers, become their own boss, write books (see what I did there…?) and generally look danger in the face and laugh out loud. These are the people who, as The Script say, *walk straight through Hell with a smile.* They wear a t shirt saying 'so what?' and they do what they want anyway. Maybe sometimes we have to go through some harsh lessons to arrive at this mind-set. Some will be born with it. Some will work for it. Some will never, ever get it. May they sit forever comfortable in their personally moulded arse shaped cushion on their sofa to the front of the wide screen TV that they worship. Good luck to them inside their bubble.

I mentioned the Nike advertising campaign earlier and it is worth mentioning again. For many years Nike would advertise their trainers on TV without ever actually mentioning their product. I mean, it's a shoe. Just a shoe! You stick it on your foot and do stuff. It won't make you the best in the world and it won't set your world on fire but Nike produced one of the most successful advertising campaigns in history. How? By tapping into that emotion which keep all humans going: hope. Using a five step process they produced a series of adverts that showed an underdog, striving against the odds to be their best. Starting to reach their peak. Then they got knocked down by something; a setback. A tackle. A fall. They struggle to keep focus and ask themself, 'Can I really do this? Am I good enough?'. Then they find resolve. Fortitude. They wear determination on their face and rise like the phoenix from the ashes and battle on to the bitter end to achieve victory in whatever pursuit they have undertaken.

The shoe company that never mentioned the shoe.

So ask yourself, what do you hope for? What do you want to be? When you strip back all of the excuses and bullshit reasons why you 'can't', 'couldn't' or 'wouldn't', what is left to show that you tried your best?
I didn't try my best in the police which was a shame. So as a result I had a job which was, in a nutshell, rubbish and a bedroom in a house which was shared with a few mates. I had fallen from starting a decent career in a thriving town with prospects to having a crappy job living in student accommodation and, might I add, my life was not the same as it had been before because everyone else had progressed with their life and moved on! So I fucked up there.

It did mean I was back in the same town as my Taekwon-Do instructor though and it wasn't long after I returned to Bedford that I started a more regular training routine with him again. I had no gym membership and couldn't afford one so it was Taekwon-Do or nothing.

My time in the police (and for the fourteen months prior to joining) had been a time of weight lifting. I had put on some solid muscle and was young enough to have weathered the lack of cardio enough to be able to still hold my own during the Taekwon-Do sessions. However I had started smoking again which was a habit that blighted my ability. At this time it must have been about £4.50 for a pack of twenty of my chosen brand (I won't mention which because I wouldn't want my millions of worldwide fans to try and be me and buy the same cigarettes that I bought). I settled into a routine of work and training. I had very little money apart from a small pension refund which I took and some owed holiday pay and that didn't bail me out for too long. My youthful stupidity also made itself quite known when, having walked past a car forecourt whilst walking to work for the umpteenth time, I could no longer resist the Ford Escort 1.6Si in pepper red that kept asking me to buy it.

Despite having a sketchy creditworthiness the sales rep still managed to find me a finance package (wasn't he amazing) and I bought a car for £9000 worth about £5,995. I loved the car though.

So I had time to train and a car. Life was okay. I had even passed a couple of grading exams in Taekwon-Do and had reached the infamous level of blue belt. This is where most people stay for years on end and either leave completely or start another martial art which they think is easier. It represents having trained for long enough to have learned some cool stuff but realise that black belt is still quite a journey and tends to make or break the student. Blue belt was a nemesis to be defeated.

Although training was good I was floating somewhat and decided that I needed direction. In a moment of clarity it seemed a sensible idea to look for employment in the fitness industry. After all, I had a degree in sport, my fitness instructor award and plenty of experience. It would be perfect for me if I could train other people to enjoy the benefits of exercise which I have experienced over the years.

I came across a job at an independent gym about fifteen miles from Bedford in a village in central Bedfordshire. A chap had decided to lease a building within the ground of a golf club to start a fitness centre. It wasn't the newest of buildings and was in poor repair inside and out. The two floors consisted of peeling walls and gently undulating floors. There were changing rooms which were full of rubbish and wood and a wet area which would require a strong, industrial fungicide before being decorated and opened. The downstairs floor would serve as the gym, studio, and wet area with sauna, steam room and hot tub and changing facilities. The upstairs area would be a beauty therapy area where ladies would come for spa days. The golf club would provide food at a nominal cost to the club as part of the packages.

I was employed as head (the only) gym instructor and would be in charge of inductions, programmes, setting up a weekly timetable of studio classes and maintenance of the gym and wet area.

It was a much better environment to be in although the pay was not exactly brilliant compared to my last job. Still, at least I had access to a gym for free and was in a more motivational environment. I was not a particularly strong minded person and surrounding myself in what I believed to be a positive environment was a good move for me. Everyone in life should strive to be around positive people, uplifting experiences and encouraging personalities. We feed off of our environment and we create that environment within which we exist and so we are completely responsible for this part of our lives.

The gym was a ladies gym. Let's just deal with the obvious right away shall we? The fact that I was a young male in a ladies gym probably conjures up images that would result in any young male reading this book to require an imminent cold shower. Allow me to burst your bubble. Most of the ladies at the gym (who were lovely people by the way) were fairly well off and advancing somewhat in age compared to me. Some wanted to be really fit and healthy. Some were passing the time whilst the men played golf. Others openly admitted that they simply liked the undivided attention of a young man and would happily pay extra for personal training for this. They would turn up with their 'just out of the salon' hair style, make up applies with the strongest aroma of perfume meaning that anyone who smoked within 100 metres of the building were putting us all in danger. So it wasn't quite the environment which you might be imagining.

The facilities were not as I had experienced before either. Having come from a gym in Watford that contained solid, cast iron plates and plenty of free weights, the owner of this gym had purchased some hydraulic resistance machines which were all hooked up to this network of tubes that ran around the edge of the room. You would press a button to inflate the pressure gauges in the machine to the equivalent of a certain poundage and then another button to deflate it and reduce the poundage. Many a laugh was had as the ladies would decrease the weights as air escaped from the machines in various tones. These were resistance machines designed for rehabilitation purposes. They were not what a young male would have chosen to use but they were all that was available. And there were only about 10 machines in the gym too. That was it. It was not a large, commercial gym so much as a local, select place. Regardless I would stay after hours to work out or take the opportunity during the quite hours to the same effect.

Although it wasn't perfect the fact that I was the only instructor at the gym gave me a chance to do whatever I wanted. The owner considered himself a businessman but was not adept in fitness at all. This was evident by his proportions. So he trusted me to manage the gym and classes. I was not trained to do any fitness classes so I had to use a bit of creative thinking. Sometimes on the journey of life you are taken on a small detour and although you know you will join the main path soon you have to navigate through unknown territory for a while. Just like I adapted my own workouts to use hydraulic resistance machines, I used whatever knowledge I could find in the library of my mind to piece together some classes which I though the ladies might enjoy.

I knew how to set up a fitness circuit and so used my knowledge to put a 10 station circuit together that would be relevant for the ladies. I had dumbbells, inflatable balls, mats and large elastic bands to use now too and put myself through a workout to see how hard it was and how long it would last including a warm up and a cool down.

At this time of my life I had several experience in martial arts (Karate and Taekwon-Do) and so I put together a 'martial arts to music' class. Familiar names would be Tae-Bo or Boxercise and I created a brand for our club called Kick Blitz. I work in advertising and marketing during the day and looking back I can chuckle to myself when I see what I did. It was never going to go global I'll put it that way! It used very basic kicks and punches which is fine but I had no qualification in aerobics or exercising to music so I had to go through the workout myself to test it. I can imagine I looked like the male version of Geri Haliwell in her video for 'It's Raining Men' in the dance studio only not quite as graceful!

I also thought I would offer some personal tuition in martial arts too. The owner of the gym was fine with this and even bought a couple of cheap focus pads and boxing gloves for me to use. After all, the more he could offer to his clients, the more likely they were to spend money and stay at the gym.

I look back and I can see what I was trying to do now. Here I was, a young man, being trusted to offer a great range of services to paying customers. Although I loved martial arts and wanted to progress I saw an opportunity to put myself on a pedestal that was not finished being built yet. I had no business offering tuition in a martial art. I had not passed my black belt or taken an instructor qualification. I took the opportunity simply because the opportunity was there to be taken but it would not make me who I wanted to be. My ego made my decision for me. I wanted a position of importance and was in a place where no one would question my ability. No one would ask for certification. Ladies would pay me to learn and I fed off of their lack of knowledge to engineer this position for myself.

I only had a few clients and it didn't really last too long. I don't feel ashamed if what I did. I was a young man trying to find my place and made a bad decision. I would say, however, that I was *lucky* that no one got hurt as I am sure I would not have been insured to teach a martial art in the gym. I gave a few people a good workout and only stuck to really basic moves and combination. Once a second instructor was hired he brought experience of aerobics and all those other classes which ladies preferred so I wrapped up my classes and concentrated on the gym.

Valuable lesson though.

I knew I wasn't ready. I taught anyway but kept to basics in a bad attempt to convince myself that my instructor or seniors would be OK with what I was doing. I had a phobia about black belts- the belt itself that is. I would never touch a black belt or put one around my waist until I had earned my own. That would be incredibly bad karma in my eyes. I kept that belief right up until I passed my black belt and I know that deep down I'm a good person. This was a wrong turning on my journey and I soon found my way back onto the right path. But consider someone who does not have these scruples:

Joe has a few years' experience in karate. Joe comes to believe that he can handle himself and that it's pointless learning a few extra kata or combinations to earn his black belt with this association. After all, who are they to tell Joe he is worthy of a black belt? Joe could probably take their head guys anyway, couldn't he? Half of them are too old to fight anyway!

Joe decides that, as he is now a complete fighter he deserves a black belt. So how can he do this? In fact, why can't *he do this?!*

So Joe decides to 'invent' his own martial art and gives it a funky name: No Can Do. He goes to the local sports shop and buys himself a plain white outfit and a black belt for thirty quid. Joe goes home, puts it on and looks in the mirror. Now he is a black belt. He throws a few punches at himself in the mirror and gives himself a glare to prove to himself he is a black belt.

Joe sits down, has a cup of crouching tiger green leaf tea (black belts drink this kind of stuff out of small white cups with no handles) and ponders what to do now. Joe is a black belt. But no one knows it. Joe needs people to realise that he is a black belt as this will further feed his ego and prove that he is worthy. Joe should open a club! That's what he should do! He could teach people No Can Do and once they learn what can be achieved after training at the local club once a week for a few years they too could be as great as him! If he started a club with a beginner's course then he would be certain that he would be better than anyone who joined anyway so his new white belts would think he is awesome.

Joe hires a hall and hands some flyers out. He sets up a free website and email account (NoCanDo@gmail.com), contacts some suppliers to get prices of outfits, knocks up some cheap certificates that he can use for grading tests and even a club membership form.

And so Joe starts his class.....

I wonder how familiar this sounds to people. I see it every week in every town. There is nothing illegal about what Joe has done. Joe has put together his own syllabus and named it so Joe owns it. Joe can put a black belt around his waist if he want. But as yet there are a few things that Joe hasn't done. Joe isn't insured or licensed. No association recognises Joe's black belt. Joe also has no experience teaching. Joe's story is a familiar one about people who need to inflate their egos and feel important for the wrong reasons. This can be because they lack something in their lives, see the martial arts as a way to make money through deceiving people who are not informed or are ignorant of what it means to actually work hard for something in their life. The extent to which they can go can be frightening too. Let's continue with Joe's story:

Joe paces nervously in his community centre dojo. It is twenty minutes until his first class. He is moment away from revealing No Can Do to the world. The doubt creeps into his mind: will his new students look up to him? What if they question his skill? What if they want to fight with him? Then Joe gives himself a mental slap around the face. No! He had experience dammit! He handled himself against people in his old class for over 2 years and he still knew he could take the old guys who headed up the association. No one questioned them *so why would anyone question Joe?! (Joe's old association had written to Joe as his license had run out and was due for renewal but Joe ignored it. He was the boss now).*

Joe looked over to the corner of the room: there was a table with some enrolment forms, business cards and even some signage that he had got printed up. It looked like a tidy display. Very professional. The logo that Joe got through a website company was worth £10 too. Joe had got his logo embroidered onto his gi (white karate outfit) too. No one would question him about being legit.

Five minutes before lesson time.

People were turning up! Some had brought the flyers that Joe had delivered. Some were empty handed but maybe they saw the small ad from the local newspaper. Either way Joe has customers.... STUDENTS! I mean students.

Joe started his lesson with a welcome and an introduction. Very professional. He didn't mention about his last club. That wasn't necessary. Suffice to say he was a black belt and was looking forward to helping these people learn self-defence and maybe even earn a black belt of their own.

His lesson covered a basic warm up, one punch, one kick and a little fitness. Joe had booked the hall for enough time to answer any questions after class and for people to complete the enrolment forms. Everything was going great....

So from here nothing looks untoward so far. An opening event is happening. People turn up. They learn stuff that is basic but appropriate which is normal. They choose to enrol.
Option 1:

...the next week Joe turns up to his hall and there are ten people waiting for him! They signed up last week. Joe's class was up and running! He had his first ten people to teach. Joe started making plans to buy outfits for them with his embroidered logo. They would buy these and really feel part of the No Can Do family.

This could be the start of a club that churns out a watered down style with black belts who think they are good but are not. It probably won't even be their fault as they will not experience any other club, style or competition. Joe might say that they don't enter sporting events as their art is deadly and they could kill someone.

Option 2:

After the opening class Joe invites people to the corner table to get some more information, to enrol and to ask any questions that they needed answering. Joe was a bit nervous about this bit. He didn't want anyone asking something awkward as his old instructor used to handle the admin but he knew he had to speak with people to get some students enrolled.

One lad who was about fifteen years old had come with his parents. It was clear to see that the lad had no martial experience and little strength and coordination. He was quiet and clearly shy. Truth be told it was his dad who had made him come in an attempt to get his son to 'man up' a bit. Joe really wanted him to sign up- he was exactly the sort of beginner that Joe wanted to teach.

Joe greeted them at his table and asked if the lad would be signing up. 'Yes he will,' said the dad firmly, 'he needs something like this. I just wanted to ask you something first though. I used to do a bit of judo years ago. We were affiliated to the UK Judo Federation. Who are you affiliated too?'

This would not be a good time for Joe.

The dad knows about martial arts and national governing bodies etc. If Joe lies he runs the risk of being checked up on and then he will be exposed for lying. If he tells the truth he will probably say *'We're not affiliated to anyone else. We're independent. I don't like the politics of big associations.'*. Nothing legally wrong with that. What it does mean, though, is that if someone grades in No Can Do then their belt will not be recognised by any other club or style anywhere. It will only be a black belt within your own group which, in this case, is headed up by Joe the failed karate student. Furthermore, Pushy Dad may then say *'How much is your license and insurance?'* License & Insurance?! Shit! Joe hadn't thought of that! Now he was in trouble. This could be a reason for the club to close before it had even started.

However, Joe might have thought of this in part:

A week before the class is due to start, Joe contacts some insurance companies off of the internet. He asked whether they can help: he is a karate instructor starting a class and needs some level of insurance, what can they offer? They tell him about public liability, something called indemnity and asks if he will insure his students for accident and injury too? Joe asks how much it costs because he doesn't have much cash right now. After getting some prices he decides to take insurance for himself even though it will cost him about £100 and will wait for other insurances. He just wouldn't let the students spar for a while.

Joe doesn't consider a student having an accident in this case. Not good at all. Although nothing is stopping Joe from getting insurance for this. This would be much better but still would not detract from Joe being a fake black belt.

Licensing- this is what every student requires to be part of an association and is how your belt grading is officially recognised. So what if:

...a week before the lesson Joe sends his logo and some text to a local printer and says that he needs some small license books for his association, the International No Can Do Karate Association. It has the logo and association name on the front and inside has pages with club rules, personal details, pages for grading info and notes pages. This instructor lark is starting to cost Joe a pretty penny! He will make sure he charges a good whack to his students to cover his expenses but why not? He has spent 'years' learning his art and these people were lucky to be learning from a founder of a style of martial art.

Joe has thought of a lot of things. It's getting harder and harder to tell if he is a fake club or not and his actions are really drawing him into his own little martial bubble. Joe will by now firmly believe that he is an amazing master of his own art. He won't be talked around by reason or justified argument. I've even seen some people change their name and introduce themselves as 'Master XXX' or an Oriental sounding name. Joe now has a business and is not doing anything illegal.

What Joe has done is water down an existing syllabus so that whoever is the first to reach their black belt in No Can Do is not going to be very good at all because the real knowledge is not there. So when push comes to shove and that black belt in No Can Do is attacked for real he will get his arse handed to him on a plate and wonder why. From there he can look forward to anger, resentment, bitterness, confusion, self-esteem issues, depression and other possible results. In this case the student has been filled with false hope and a false belief that what they know is a complete system and that they have the experience and knowledge to deal with a situation. Unfortunately this is very common indeed.

I am glad that I did not try to push this limit all those years ago. I persisted and achieved my black belt after thirteen years of training. At the time of writing this I am now a 3rd degree black belt but do not believe for one second that the colour or rank number of belt around the waist is indicative of the skill level of the wearer. That is no longer the case. Why? Because there are too many out there who have broken away from the norm without proper knowledge and ability to produce a black belt of the standard that they were before. You may ask, 'why should I bother grading if the belt doesn't make me a better fighter?' A few possible answers would be: personal pride, accomplishment, achievement, reach a life goal. It is still a commendable and difficult achievement to earn a real black belt in a martial or combat style and an amazing journey. All I would say is that once you have reached the level of 1st degree black belt, do not see that as the end of the journey. You may have reached one destination but you will then need to start a new journey to a whole new place. I once heard a black belt described as a good indication that the wearer could probably hold their own against a single opponent. I quite like this as an explanation (assuming the black belt is a proper one). The journey from there provides experience and further knowledge on other areas like multiple attacks, weapons and more. It is also important to consider the psychological aspects of confrontation and there are precious few schools that deal with this part of the package too, believe me.

So take your time on your journey. Enjoy it. Anyone can buy a black belt. Not everyone truly earns it though.

So the gym had given me a little direction. After joining the police I had started smoking again and as yet had not broken free of this habit. This was about to become a problem in my life that would take several more years to conquer. Another event was around the corner too that would permanently divert my route in life.

Chapter Five
Kids and drugs

Success and money have nothing in common

Although I was working I was not financially coping. I had recently bought a car on finance (stupidly) and did not know how to properly balance income and expenditure. Rather than spending sensibly, budgeting and tackling things head on I decided to take a second job driving a taxi on the weekend. There was a local company that was managed by a friend's dad so I was able to slide into the job without needing to worry about silly things like a taxi license or training. Friday and Saturday evenings I would work until the early hours making cash in hand to help out with the bills. Sometimes I would work until it got light, especially if there was a really early airport run to do. I could make fifty quid on that job alone sometimes. I would hand my keys in to the office, wearily drive home and collapse on my bed tired but happy in the knowledge I was earning extra money and not out spending it.

Sometimes in life you have to do what it takes to get by. I have two jobs right now in life. My day job is online marketing and advertising and I teach martial arts in my schools in the evening and at weekends. Why? Because I have a mortgage, a family to support and I love martial arts and that is the best option right now. Self-respect is all about taking responsibility for what you do and always trying your best and if that means you need to work more to earn more than so be it. I didn't want to reduce my standard of living so I got another job.

As any taxi drivers may tell you there are certain perks of driving a taxi. One of those perks would be the many young ladies that you pick up and, being the young stag that I was, I would sometimes get attention. It couldn't be helped. I guess I'm just easy on the eye.

One evening I was called to the office to pick up two ladies (and a random drunk bloke) and take them back from the local club to a couple of neighbouring towns. The random drunk was just sharing the taxi and was luckily dropped in the first town without redecorating the back seat of the car. The two ladies were then taken to the second town. One of the ladies was sitting next to me on the front seat and was pretty forward from the start. When I say forward I mean that she did, at one part of the journey, state quite clearly that she was going to bite me and bite me she did.

She had long dark hair, dark eyes and everything she wore was black. Black leather jacket. Black skirt. Black high boots. Under that jacket lay a portfolio of tattoos covering her back and arm- an expression of her life and personality. She told me her name It sounded Italian. We exchanged numbers (she took my phone and put her number in it and told me to call her) and I dropped them off to carry on with my shift.

For the remaining few hours of my shift she would regularly text me and tell me to come over straight away. I needed to finish my shift. I needed the money. I did reassure her that I would come over after I had slept though.

As the sun came up in Bedford I dropped my keys in to the office and walked back to my own car near the local park. The air was cold and fresh and was the only thing keeping me awake. I drove the mile to my house with the window open, went inside and fell on my bed.

Several hours later I woke to my phone vibrating. It was the girl from last night. She was texting me again. I guess I was late. Suffice to say I needed to freshen up and we arranged to meet that evening at a pub near Luton where she lived with her friend from the taxi.

It had been some time since a girl had given me much interest and I cannot deny that I was somewhat flattered. I was determined to follow this through and see what happened despite being nervous and shy around women in general.

Besides it gave me a good opportunity to give my new car a bit of a drive and show it off to someone.

I picked her up in Luton town centre and we drove to this pub at the side of a main road. I couldn't say why we went there. It just happened to be where we stopped. We had a drink. We played pool. We smoked. She also had some pot which we smoked. I had spent years smoking pot in my teenage years and early twenties and it didn't take much persuasion for the 'sheep' side of my personality to appear. In hindsight I should have never started down that route again but I had little will power for someone who wanted so badly to be the best I could be. I still didn't know myself. I still didn't know my identity.

From there we met most days. The gym where I worked was roughly half way between my house and hers so I would drive to her place after work, spend the evening mostly smoking cheap weed with her and her mate, sleep there and go to work in the morning. Life carried on that way for a while. Smoking weed has a habit of drawing you in to its world and after some time the norm becomes being stoned and the sobriety that is felt after sleeping becomes alien. For a couple of months we continued on this cycle of staying in and smoking weed which was interspersed with me working and occasionally going home to wash clothes and collect items that I needed.

It would take me several more years to shake the habit of smoking weed and cigarettes but I would say now that I lay no blame to anyone but myself for my bad habits. At times I have chosen to blame others for my short comings. I blamed that girl from the taxi for some time for getting back into smoking weed. I've blamed others for me smoking. I've blamed everyone but myself for this and for messing up other areas of my life. Life has taught me how to be responsible though and this is all part of my journey to black belt. It's on me and always has been. Everyone has a choice in life for everything that they do and I have chosen to do these things which have held me back. In turn I have broken free of my vices and learned from the experience. I could argue that without being weak I would not have learned how to be strong. In my own way I broke myself down to my lowest point and needed things to be bad in order for me to realise that I needed to make things better.

After a couple of months of my herbally infused lifestyle I got a text message telling me that I didn't actually have a girlfriend because she wasn't ready for a relationship. She had only recently finished with her previous boyfriend and just wanted to be mates. I was annoyed but not completely dejected. I didn't love her. The feelings did not run that deep at that time. My reply was simply that life goes on and that I did not want to be mates. Don't text. Don't call. Good luck with life.

And that was that.

Until I got a text.

She needed to talk with me. She was a highly individual person who did not easily show reliance on anyone else and knowing her as I did at that time I assumed that this was important. She certainly wasn't the type to change her mind and try to rekindle anything. I thought about what she could want to talk about and honestly the only two things I could come up with were that she was HIV positive and needed to tell me or that she was pregnant.

I phoned her at a moment when the gym was empty. I was the only person there. The boss was out. No clients were in. I had time. I went outside and dialled her number. I don't think my heart had ever beaten against my chest so hard in my life.

She was pregnant.

Either way it was going to be a bomb shell but I was sure I had the much better choice of the two possible outcomes that I had thought of.

I still went white as a sheet. I was not prepared for parenthood although I was not afraid of actually being a father.

For the purpose of humour might I add right now that as she told me she was pregnant the song 'Mamma Told Me Not To Come' by Tom Jones was blaring out of the gym stereo. This is priceless. I still laugh at this fact.

We agreed to talk and I headed over to her place after work. Stepping back into her mate's house where she lived was somewhat awkward.

We smoked some weed....

We agreed to try again. Give it another go. Maybe we could learn to love each other and bring our child up. Suffice to say I was not excluded from the start and began to feel a bit optimistic. I had no idea how I would support a family or how to be a parent but I was going to give it a bloody good shot.

It wasn't long before she decided again that she didn't actually want a relationship but that we would be friends and still bring up our child. She did not want to lose control of this life changing event. She felt a need to control every aspect of her life and needed independence for her identity. There was no point in arguing with her. Once she made her mind up she would not be persuaded to change her opinion. Rather now than several years down the line.

She wanted to try and move to Bedford though to bring our child up in a nicer place than Luton. I was pleased about this and agreed to help in any way that I could.

There wasn't really much I could do to help apart from some moral support I guess. She did eventually move over to Bedford and I tried my best to support her through the pregnancy and beyond and the result today is a healthy and flourishing twelve year old girl.

Over the years we have taken each other to hell and back though. I could, if choosing, write a massive section of this book based around why I believe that everything was her fault and not mine; about why I was in the right and she was in the wrong. I won't though. Suffice to say that: yes, I have tried my best over the years and I have made difficult decisions (and still do) based on what I genuinely believe are in the best interest of my child. I sleep well at night in the knowledge that I can justify my choices and decision and have remained steadfast and not strayed from the path of parenthood in order to bring up my eldest daughter to the best of my ability. Any wrongdoings on my part have (hopefully) been acknowledged and accepted and I have forgiven myself for them and moved on. People do makes mistakes in life. I believe that the course of action you take after recognising a mistake is more important in progressing in life and working towards reaching your potential.

Jazmine was a beautiful baby.
Affectionately named 'Squeaky' on account of the squeaking noise she made as a baby, she has a shock of jet black hair that would later turn dark blonde and later be dyed black again, then a chunk shaved off as she tried to discover her near teenage identity. During her first few months I didn't work much. Things had gone very wrong at the gym where I had worked forcing me to leave without having received my pay. It took several weeks to get the money which was owed to me and this started a downward spiral with finances that I would eventually fail completely to solve.
Jazmine and I bonded well. Throughout all the years of trials and tribulations, affection and dislike, arguments and agreements, I have always been one hundred per cent confident in our relationship and I know that my actions towards my eldest are always in her best interest.
For a while though I would be destined to spend time with my daughter, drive a taxi from time to time and smoke weed.

Let's address weed shall we.
Weed is an addictive drug.
You can smoke it in a joint, a pipe, put it in a bong, A-bomb, bucket, ice bucket, in a frozen pint glass, blow back, bake it in a cake or sprinkle it over your fucking salad if you prefer. It comes as a bud, solid, liquid or oil and has names like Rocky,

Slate, Skunk, Northern Lights, Purple Haze, Shit and various others. Suffice to say when ingested using the desired method it induces a state of mind that is euphoric, makes you light headed and in my case would aim to put all of life's troubles very firmly on another plane so that I had no worries at all. It removes you from normal life. It also makes you rather hungry and can dry your mouth out so refreshments are usually present during a session amongst seasoned smokers.

My experience with weed (or whatever you want to call it) lasted many years and it takes over your life given half the chance. It certainly took over mine.

Pot smokers form an invisibly bound cult with common rituals and practices. Pot smokers who have never met could meet each other for a smoking session and all have the same modes of etiquette and behaviours all of which seem to bind the smokers together to provide an atmosphere of community, acceptance and belonging. Roller's rights meant if you rolled the joint then you had first smoke. It was polite to pass the dragon around mates if everyone else was doing so. In some smoking sessions I went to, the only rule was that you provided something to smoke. How much was up to the individual and everyone was trusted to provide what they could. All the pot would then be piled high in the middle for anyone to use and the bigger the pile the better the camaraderie of the smokers who were present.

Some people (usually potheads) say smoking is not addictive. They could stop whenever they wanted but they did not want to stop. They enjoyed smoking pot. *If* and *when* they wanted to give up then they would.

What a fucking joke.

The level of self-delusion that potheads have is beyond annoying and I speak from personal experience.

I have no problem with people wanting to escape the regular troubles of life. Life can be stressful. Life can deal you a crap hand and everyone needs a break. People have a drink, smoke or go a few rounds on the bag to relieve stress. But nothing rivals the extent of escapism that I've witnessed from potheads apart from harder drug users.

CANNABIS IS ADDICTIVE.

Yes it is! It takes over your life and is extremely hard to give up so, if you are reading this and have been smoking pot for a while and are still saying it isn't addictive:

YOU'RE NOT KIDDING ANYONE!

Wake up mate, you're a fucking pothead and you're addicted! I feel strongly about this as I lost several years of my life to a green cloudy haze.

So I ask, if you use drugs or drink alcohol, what are you running from? What are you avoiding and do not have the bottle to face up to? There's no point in fluffing this up- why would someone feel the need to escape their regular life *so much* that they end up believing that being stoned is normal and that being sober is to be avoided at all cost.

Smoking provides escape... from what? Relationship problems? financial difficulty? Health issues? Mental issues? I am sure that occasionally someone can feel physical pain relief using cannabis (there is a big argument going on about cannabis use in the UFC right now by top level MMA athletes) but the majority of the time underlying reasons for escapism need to be identified, discussed and dealt with head on. It is a brave step to admit a fault or a problem and to ask for help (even if you are asking yourself or God for strength) and all excuses will make themselves known, fuelled by the pothead monkey on your shoulder who will try to convince you to keep smoking the evil weed.

"I don't want to give up, I like it". "I'm not addicted." "It helps me to relax." "It relieves my stress."

I ask you this: what do you think all the non-smokers do to deal with stress, life or other problems? Before a cigarette smoker became reliant on tobacco to relieve stress they dealt with it in another way. Before the alcoholic used alcohol to escape life's troubles they dealt with things another way (maybe a long time ago but they did) and all those who have recovered from addiction have proved their ability to cope too.

I used cannabis to mask the issues of life for years. I have family who may only realise this fact once this book is published and they read it because I still have not found a need or desire to share this fact with them. If you have just found this out, well now you know. Some will be surprised by my past. Some will not. Some will have contributed to what I have been through. Some will not care. It's not for me to elaborate here. It's in the past because I chose to move on, thank God so please don't dwell on it.

A lot of my worried were borne out of naivety. I had mounting financial trouble amongst other things. It had been building up for years without me knowing.

When I left home for university in 1996 a red, plastic credit card arrived for me in the post one day with a £3000 limit. I don't ever remembering asking for it and I was so naive I had to call the bank to ask what it was for. I had a cheque book too. I had savings, a small salary, loans and grants and no one to tell me how to handle it. I was too weak to control myself and the inevitable did happen.

A while after Jazmine was born I decided that I needed to sort my life out a bit and managed to secure a job in a finance house. This was like a bank only they were phasing out their current accounts and concentrating on consolidation loans, shop finance and insurances like PPI, accident covers and household insurance. I was a customer service manager and I learned how to look at people's finances and offer them loans to consolidate their existing debt into one, easy, 'affordable' monthly payment. I was very good at it too. With the ability to 'speak the speak' and knowing how to relate to people with debt I quickly rose to being one of the best sellers in the region and I was earning good money in bonuses. Regional managers were pleased and used a few of us to form an elite sales team to travel over the region and train those who might be struggling to sell as much as we did.

This was the harder end of sales. We were lending up to £75,000 secured and £15,000 unsecured and interest rates could be higher than 40% APR. I was a seller in subprime finance. It was not the most ethical of practices but I didn't care. I was good at what I did and respected within the company. I was, however, still naive in finance. I was earning money but was spending too much and my debt was growing instead of decreasing.

Even after I made it to branch manager after a couple of years I was not in a better position. The company had screwed me over by not increasing my salary only now, instead of earning my bonus, I could not as I was not a seller. I was a manager. I should not have taken that role based on my own finances but I was blinded by false prestige of being able to say I was a bank manager.

After a while struggling on I was offered a position in a high street bank as an account manager. This move would take me from subprime lending to high street banking and would be more respectable although I would lose my company car. My own car has been taken back by the finance company a while back as I could not afford it and I had been relying on a company car as a branch manager so I would have to deal with no transportation of my own. No matter. The bank was in the High Street and I lived in a street just off the top of the High Street. I could walk to work in 10 minutes.

My old bank did try to keep me. We went out for a team night out where the area manager got inebriated and promised me a higher salary and to backdate what was owed. It was all a bit cringey and was too little too late. I had had enough of subprime lending. Everyone was trying to be something that they weren't. Team nights out would be alcohol and drug fuelled events which ended up in strip clubs with £350 bottles of Cristal champagne, cigars and lap dances. Extravagance would be bought on credit which would be stretched to it's capacity but not openly mentioned for fear of looking financially weak. We were lending big bucks! We all gave the impression of being well off when we weren't and it was the undoing of a lot of people. Not long after leaving for the high street bank my old company ended up shutting over 200 branches nationwide, even after being bought out by the HSBC group. I wonder whether it was due to unethical practices but I will never know.

I carried on in high street banking for a while. I was still a pothead and would wake up, smoke a joint, walk to work for a cup of cardboard coffee, muddle through my day and come home to more pot. I skipped breakfast. I ate rubbish for lunch. I was barely training. I even had a couple of smoking buddies from the Taekwon-Do club who would come round for a smoke rather than train. My life was being consumed by the cult of weed.

The problem was my smoking meant that I was not addressing the ever growing pile of bills and reminders that were growing in my post box at the front of the flats where I lived. I had gotten too used to receiving letters from debt management companies and banks and the longer it went on the more I believed that I was not a good person and did not deserve nice things or even food on the table. From time to time the post box would get so full that my mail would be poking out of the letter box and only then would I prepare myself to open what was inside. This usually involved a ritual of rolling two large joints. I would smoke one before getting the post to take the edge off of my nerves. Then I would gather up the reams of paper and envelopes from the mail box, stagger back to my studio flat and deposit the pile on one end of the sofa.

Then I would spark up the other joint.

The first job would be to remove anything that was not important to me: flyers, menus, junk mail, Sky and Virgin offers. That usually shrunk the pile down nicely. I would then look for familiar envelopes. I would be able to identify which letters would relate to which debt by the return address of which collection company had sent them. I would know the names of the people to speak with and what the next letter would say when it would be sent the next month. Letters from agencies would go in a pile and then I would seek out anything that required immediate attention: bank letters and council tax letters. Once opened and I knew the full extent of the damage I would continue smoking the remaining joint to further calm my nerves. A plan would be formulated in my mind as to who to call from work tomorrow (Calling from work was good because the manager would leave you alone if he looked through the glass fronted offices and see you calling people. He thought you were selling something).

How I managed to survive for so long like this is beyond me. I must have ducked and dived more times than Del Boy from Only Fools and Horses. I shudder when I remember the stress and anxiety which had built up over the years from this lifestyle and I am relieved not to be there anymore.

Training was now non-existent. Life was consumed with worrying about finance. I was constantly working out how to find cash to buy food, how to stave off some debt collector or another, trying to fund my pot habit and counting down the days until pay day until I reached a point in my life where I had been before.

105

Something had to give.

I fell behind with one too many payments. I thought I had planned right but somehow I'd forgotten about a bank loan that I had been paying off for a few years. The backlash of it was a fine for an unpaid direct debit and an outstanding debt that would use money that was allocated for something else and within me I knew it was the end. Family had bailed me out of a few situations before but had never known the extent of my debt. I used cards and overdrafts to move money around to pay bills but everything was now maxed out. I had two credit cards, three overdrafts in different banks, a bank loan, student loans, was behind with my rent and probably other things that I now cannot remember.

The bank offered me a refinance of my loan and one overdraft which meant doubling my interest rate but it was the only way to put that payment off by a few weeks. It also meant another couple of years on the terms of the repayments. I had had this for years now and I was done. Enough was enough and I couldn't cope.

The next day I went into my managers office to come clean. I told him that I was struggling financially and laid out on the table what my debts were. I didn't tell him exactly how far up to my neck in financial crap I was as I was too embarrassed. He made a phone call to see if the bank could do a consolidation loan for me but my credit was shocking and they flatly refused. My manager was a very matter of fact man and under FSA guidelines, I would not be able to continue doing my job lending money and offering insurance if my own finances were so bad. I was going to have to leave my job and I did not know what to do. The only advice he gave was to declare bankruptcy. I was aware of this and to have my manager recommend it was about the worst thing that I could think of. It was sound advice in hindsight but the thought of giving up on my repayments had never actually occurred to me.

I was about to reach my lowest point but they say that sometimes you have to get this low in order to start rebuilding. I had done it before. I would have to do it again.

Chapter Six
Bankrupt

When you have truly reached your lowest point in life
You can only go up.

The first step was to go to the Citizens Advise Bureau (CAB). I was an expert in dodging my finances but was a white belt when it came to dealing with them. I needed tuition. I needed guidance. I needed a fucking hard kick up the arse.

The CAB helped me to set up a plan to make token payments to all of my creditors in order to find a solution to my debt. This pissed off all of my creditors who continued to hassle me but, like the CAB advised, I would simply tell them that an offer had been made and that I was not to deviate from this no matter how much more they demanded. It provided a temporary bubble of peace around me. It was not solving my debt. It was, if anything, prolonging the repayments. But it meant I had some calm. I was advised to put what money I had into a separate account. I had a spare one from working at the bank (I was still working notice with them although not with the public anymore). It was a painful few weeks of demeaning work around suspicious colleagues and I had no spare cash for pot or decent food. This had to be done though. If I didn't deal with this now I felt that I would be living this life until the day I died (which seemed to be getting closer and closer. I was now smoking holding my asthma reliever spray in my hand as the constant smoking and stress was giving me nightly asthma attacks).

The CAB had spoken with me about bankruptcy and, although I was nervous of doing this I spoke with my mother who agreed to pay for the process to be done. It was the ultimate hypocrisy and last undignified act to have to rely on my own mother to pay for me to declare myself bankrupt but that is what I did.

In July of 2007 Bedford County Court declared me financially bankrupt without even calling me into the courtroom. This accolade was placed in the public newspaper in the public notices section. I still have that cut out.

I knew that going bankrupt would be a monumental and pivotal point in my life and I had begun to prepare for court several weeks earlier. I had started working for a good friend of mine (Shez, I love you man) as a drainage engineer (shit shifter) and had swapped smoking pot and cigarettes for bags of carrot sticks. I would lose my flat as the rental debt would be wiped clean as part of my bankruptcy and would be sleeping on lounge floors for a while before finding a room to illegally rent in a one bedroom DSS council flat. But as I walked out of that courtroom I remember feeling about as alive as I had felt for many years. A huge weight had been lifted off of my shoulders and I felt tension leave my body. Apart from my student loans which did not yet need to be addressed I had no financial debt. I had a job and roof over my head and my salary was to be my own. I had to be careful as I could be liable to pay some of the debt back for twelve months after being declared bankrupt but with all my experience of ducking and diving I would pass the next year without paying back anything.

Life changed for me after that day. I had learned my lesson with finance. I had no credit and just a basic cash card bank account. I had no way of obtaining debt or finance and would learn to live with what money I had.
I had also successfully broken free of smoking.
After all those years of trying I had found a good time to have the strength to give up. My lungs were feeling the benefit and bland foods like rice and potatoes started to taste vibrant again. I had also started training regularly again as I now had the time, energy and money to do the lessons. Giving up smoking had a profound effect on my energy during Taekwon-Do lessons and others in the class would comment about how much sharper I was and how long I could spar for. I had been greeted by my instructor and colleagues like an old friend and they made me feel as welcome as they had always done. Maybe they had sensed that my life was on a roller coaster and were pleased that I had found some direction again in life. I never came clean to

my instructor about my smoking and debt. The embarrassment was too much for me. I'm sure he will read this book once it is published so I can take this opportunity to publicly say: I'm sorry. I'm sorry for letting you and me down. I'm sorry I did not learn my lesson sooner and I am sorry that I was seduced by impure and illegal substances when you tried so hard to help us to better ourselves. And I thank God that I was able to find the strength to rebuild my life and will take this opportunity to try to help others to reach their potential in life just like you tried to help me.

It was getting hard to keep away from pot. The guy I rented a room from was a habitual smoker. I had smoked with him before giving up and if I thought that I was a heavy smoker then I would learn with him what a heavy smoker could really smoke. It was a bit frustrating as I was now clean of smoking and wanted to be rid of the negative impact of it altogether. The dreaded weed had already taken more of my time than I cared to remember and I didn't want my clothes and Taekwon-Do outfit smelling of it too. I was paranoid.

The flats where we lived were likened to Beirut. Positioned halfway down a side street from a main road they housed life's drop outs. Inhabitants were mainly on benefits and drugs were easy to come by. One weekend when my house mate had his three children staying and I had Jazmine, we all had to evacuate the flat as the flat downstairs and to the side of ours had been set on fire. Rumour has it that the man living there was a paedophile. I was okay there though as my house mate had lived there a while. Also I was a drainage engineer so I did a real man's job. I drove a van, wore shitty clothes and generally fit the right image of what was expected.

Training was going well. I had been working hard at my Taekwon-Do and even graded a couple of times. I was fast approaching the colour black on my belt and was beginning to think that it was possible to be a black belt after all. Several students in the club had commented that my energy levels had markedly improved since giving up smoking. They were right. I had felt the surges of energy in my muscles since I had stopped polluting them with poisons.

Training was going well. Finance was being managed. I had stopped smoking. A couple of things were about to happen that would cement my turnaround in life towards a more positive future.

Not too long before moving to Beirut I was 'found' through social media by someone I used to know. I had a page on MySpace. At this time I was not too knowledgeable on social media but knew enough to set the page up, maintain it and understand how it worked. I was sent a message from the younger sister of someone who I used to work with. I must have had an impact on her as it was an eight or nine year gap since we had spoken and even then it was not exactly a long term, flourishing friendship. It was a fairly general, 'hey how are you' message although I was at a stage in life where a positive opportunity was absolute gold dust and I needed to surround myself with positive things.

Besides that her picture suggested that I should most definitely reciprocate!

At the time of messaging I was maybe days away from losing my internet connection at the flat where I lived (as I was essentially being evicted) and so I remember one night driving around town trying to find a computer to use for five minutes to send this girl my phone number and explain why I couldn't message through MySpace.

It was well into the night when I turned up at the working men's club where we trained on Saturday's. The regular few old men were nursing the same pints of bitter that they ordered several hours ago whilst young men battled for supremacy on the pool table. The barman was an old friend of my instructor and was a pretty laid back guy. I briefly explained my situation and asked if he had a PC that could use. He did and said it was fine for me to use it but it was a bit slow.

A bit fucking slow!?

I'm not sure how I could quantify how slow it was. For those of us old enough to remember dial-up internet no explanation is required. For those of you too young to have enjoyed this early digital era consider watching paint dry or waiting for the grass to grow. Long periods of time would pass every time a page was selected. Often times the page wouldn't successfully load and a refresh would be required.

Considering all I needed was to type in www.myspace.com then go to my message page it was the longest 45 minutes of my life. I was delighted to turn the computer off afterwards.

However, it was an important 45 minutes spent in front of a flickering screen by a small window upstairs from that club. The only other light came from a small forty watt bulb in an old, struggling lamp that had no chance of lighting anything more than three feet away from its base. I was totally focused on that screen and praying every time I clicked the button for a successful page load. I pleaded to God to successfully send the message once I had written it and once sent I slumped back in the chair slightly happier that I had managed to send my mobile number to this girl. It was up to her now of course as I did not have her number and, for all intent and purpose, no reliable internet connection either. It was well past midnight and I was not going to be graced with any text message tonight so I turned the computer off, went downstairs, thanked the barman and went home to bed.

That club on Hurst Grove in Bedford held quite a few memories for me. We trained there for several years. Unfortunately it was demolished a few years back to make way for housing. I was sad to see it go even though by that time I hadn't stepped foot inside it's doors for several years. Within those walls I had trained, taken my daughter, met the guys on stupidly early times of the morning on day long tournament expeditions, had challenges from the drunken punters and now sent a message on social media to a girl that I would eventually move in with, marry and share a beautiful baby girl.

My first date with Beckie was an interesting affair. Having successfully communicated via mobile phone for a short while we arranged to go out in Milton Keynes on a Saturday afternoon when I was not working. The set up for this first date would be different in that Jazmine(who was three at the time) would be coming with us. It was my weekend to have her to stay from her mother's house and both I and Beckie were fine with having a child come along as she was a nursery nurse and felt like Jazmine would be common ground for us and would make things easier. For transport, Beckie would pick Jazmine and me up at Beirut Towers and would drive us to the ten pin bowling alley in Milton Keynes. I couldn't drive us. I was working as a drainage engineer at the time and only had my poo van which was not for personal use. It didn't smell too good either.
I remember as she pulled up in her car that I was in luck. If nothing else then I was to get to spend the day with a really decent looking girl and have some fun with Jazmine at the same time. Although I had given up smoking a few weeks prior to this date I would not have described myself as the healthiest individual in the world. I was still coming off of the back of years of smoking weed and cigarettes and a huge amount of stress that would manifest itself in full blown depression a few years later. I was somewhat dishevelled and living in a weed filled bubble with little heating meant that I probably reeked of cannabis and damp. On the other side of the coin I was starting to exude a confidence that I had not felt in a long time. I had filed for bankruptcy at the time of our date and at this time

things were simply being processed so there was nowhere near as much pressure on me than before.

Whilst a river will emerge as a powerful torrent and flow to the sea with energy and exuberance it will always start from small rills and streams which will gain in size and momentum to create the end product. My confidence was a small rill; only starting to wend its way towards what it could potentially be but very much having started the journey nonetheless. I was able to put the troubles of life aside as a manageable task and concentrate on enjoying the day.

To look at an analogy for a moment: picture if you will a set of old fashioned scales with a central stand on which two platforms may pivot. The scales will balance when equal forces are exerted on each platform under the influence of gravity.

On one side of our metaphorical scale we place positive influences like love, happiness, potential, family, satisfaction etc. These are all the good things that encourage us through life and help us to achieve all that we desire and be all that we should be.

On the other side we place negative influences. These could be debt, poor health, anger, envy, greed, selfishness, lies etc. All those things that will, in one way or another, hold us back and be detrimental to our lives. Bad karma against good karma if you like.

We will all have positive and negative influences in our lives. It is what we do with them that matters. If we have too many negative influences in our life we worry and have lots of stress on our shoulders. This can affect our health, relationships and finances and the downwards spiral can be difficult to reverse once it gains momentum.

If we have too many positive influences in our life we can become complacent and be more susceptible to the negativity that holds us back like greed, avarice or selfishness. Eventually the scales will re-balance themselves. *We* will re-balance our selves.

There is another dimension to the scales though and that is weight. It is not enough to simply balance influencing factors. We must limit them too.

Transpose the scales to be a barbell across your shoulders. Too much weight on one side of the barbell leaves you lop sided and uncomfortable. The weight should be even. However, if there is too much weight on your shoulders, regardless of it being equal on both sides, eventually your whole being will crumble under the weight and you will be able to carry nothing.

We cannot handle an unlimited amount of stress (good or bad). We must realise what our limits are and what we can handle physically and mentally. You could owe £1000 to a bank and pay it off at £100 per month for ten months. That's achievable and realistic. But what about owing £100,000 to a bank? That's a lot more 'weight' on your shoulders. Compounded with other life issues and stresses (whether good or bad) eventually you will reach a breaking point.

You cannot handle unlimited negativity by seeking out unlimited positivity. If you believe you can I would like you to seriously consider how you place yourself in the world and what you are trying to achieve. I use money as an example as this is something that I have messed up in my past: I continually remember the phrase *you are only as rich as the spare money that you have each month after paying your bills.*

I often look at large houses with flash cars outside or those who buy designer clothes and eat out a lot and wonder how much they have to pay out each month as well as how much they earn. That detached five bedroom new build three story town house with the Jaguar on the driveway doesn't come cheap and neither are the kids' private school fees each year. Someone is earning top dollar in their job for this lot! That high flying job is going to come with a high level of stress too. The scales are balanced here but the 'weight' is heavy. Chasing salary to try to maintain lifestyle is a trap I fell into and the higher my salary the less I found myself able to deal with the stress and so I sought ways to escape the stress of life. I'm sure a lot of people out there can handle a lot of stress but the stress is still there nonetheless. Consider pictures of those who achieve the status of prime minister. The photos of them after being in office for several years are amazingly different to the pictures of them before appointment. Stress is sometimes worn like a mask for all to see and is a permanent advertisement for what happens when it gets too big.

As I write I am currently earning the highest salary in my daytime job that I have ever earned. I also make a small profit teaching my martial arts schools but now my mind-set is completely different. One of my favourite stupid quotes: *with age comes experience.* Now that I am a bit older I have a better grasp on what is required to live comfortably and happily and I no longer chase money for the same reasons that I did when I was younger. I also have very different motivations in life now; real, true motivations that are dear to my heart and a pleasure to work towards.

I had taken some steps towards re-balancing my scales.

Some of those steps have reduced the weight on top of the scales too and that release of pressure was far, far more valuable to me than the re-balancing. Without the weight a small fluctuation in equilibrium was just that: small. Balance could be easily reset by making small adjustments instead of large ones.

Back to my date.
So the day began. Since that date I have spoken with Beckie about my past in great detail. Several factors could have influenced whether or not she would even have considered a

second date. My chances of seeing her again would have been drastically reduced if:

a. I had not given up smoking
b. I had not given up smoking cannabis
c. I had entered the relationship having kept my head in the sand regarding my finances

In other words, had Beckie have contacted me on MySpace six weeks earlier, I may not be married with another daughter right now. It's amazing how much difference time can make. Things that genuinely take time should not be rushed.

As you embark upon a journey from white to black belt do not be caught up in the chase of the belt colour. Minimal times will be set between grading exams for a reason and you are free to take as much time as you need before seeking another belt as you should feel ready and worthy of wearing it. More weight should be on the shoulders of your instructor in ensuring that you have received quality tuition to be properly prepared for grading.

Be wary of schools that profess to make you a black belt in eighteen months as long as you train enough (or pay enough). You cannot buy experience and experience comes with time. The ITF Taekwon-Do syllabus states that an adult (18 years and over) must break boards when approaching higher level coloured belts and black belt. It takes time to learn not just the techniques but also the mental fortitude and physical conditioning to perform such a feat. No one who has trained for eighteen months should honestly feel comfortable undertaking this task or have enough experience in fighting, training or life in general to genuinely wear a symbol of excellence like a black belt.

Comfortable, well maintained halls and facilities are nice and all that but the end product will be determined by two things: the ability of your instructor (to teach and to undertake their art) and your commitment to learning. Concentrate on those two things, be humble and you should be fine.

Having ambition in life doesn't work unless you do.

Dealing with finances. Stopping smoking cannabis and cigarettes. Meeting Beckie. All of these things were positive influences in my life and were things that I had engineered by my own positive actions and decisions. As I reflected on where I was in my life it became evident that I was tipping the scales back in my favour and finding some balance. In the past I had achieved things that I would consider further along the timeline towards my potential but had let them slip. I had had well-paid jobs that could have been careers. I had respect from peers, family and friends through how I conducted myself. I had lived in respectable houses.

I am not a materialistic person. Far from it. My wife will confirm that simply by introducing you to my wardrobe. On the other hand my current position in life tells me that there really is nothing wrong with striving for a certain amount of financial and material respect. I have a wife and two children and therefore I have responsibilities. I am the main 'bread winner' for my family and we need a certain amount of money to survive and a certain amount of money to enjoy things. By having a good job and some spare cash I then demonstrate to my family and children what can be achieved through perseverance and hard work and instil a 'work ethic' into them. This is part of my job as a responsible parent and a work ethic is a worthy trait in the development of martial skill as well as work

As I ponder what I have had in the past and where I am in life I being to wonder what I could achieve. I had accomplished the cessation of smoking and debt and risen from the depths of being labelled 'of no fixed abode' yet I lived in a shitty DSS flat (illegally subletting) and did not have a solid career in mind. I

119

was working as a drainage engineer. This was a position that I was lucky to have as given to me by an amazing friend after I was forced to leave the banking system due to poor credit history. The job was as the title suggests: I worked in drains. I unblocked them when they got blocked. I dig them up when they collapsed or cracked. We worked on pipes, septic tanks, urinals, toilets. It was a powerfully unglamorous job and it was hard, physical graft and extremely dirty work. Same shit, different day. But this was my karma. I deserved this. It was on my shoulders that I had messed up a solid career in banking and so I welcomed the work with open arms. It was actually nice to be out of a fast paced sales environment where I could work on projects that required as much time as was necessary. We got people flowing again. We were damn good at it too! When the council boys couldn't unblock a drain it was us they called to get the job done and get it done we did. We prided ourselves on a 100% success rate of either getting it unblocked or we discovered a reason why it needed replacing. We would be out in rain, snow, hail or heavy winds at whatever hour of the day or night was required. If a pipe needed replacing we would dig like badgers for hours and hours to get to it, replace it and fill the ground in again. I can't tell you how heavy some industrial manhole covers are to lift either but on occasion they needed lifting and I didn't always have anyone else to assist. It made you tough. It was a man's job and it built me up somewhat. But it wasn't a long term career for me. It paid the bills but I felt that I needed to find a larger company to work for where doors would open and I could progress. Where I could benefit from company perks and have regular hours and earn bonuses. Something that might let me use my intellect in a different way. Something that wouldn't require Beckie hosing me down with bleach before going inside if we moved in together.
I wanted to progress.

In the martial art of Taekwon-Do we strive to live by five tenets: Courtesy, Integrity, Perseverance, Self-Control and Indomitable Spirit. At this stage I wanted to find out the meaning of perseverance. I wanted to find something that I could get better at vocationally as well as in my martial arts.

You'll find that most martial arts have a code of conduct. Some are rigid and laid out with specific words or tenets. Others have what I consider a more unwritten but generally accepted code. One of the martial arts that I study is Brazilian Jiu Jitsu. Although certain schools and associations will have rules of conduct I find that there is a general 'atmosphere' in the clubs that is different to others. Mutual respect is paramount and there is always an air of people working towards a common goal tinged with teamwork and healthy competition. I have had the same experience in MMA clubs although I know of those who have said they have found a specific MMA club to be thuggish or with arrogant brawlers. I have found more traditional classes of Karate and Taekwon-Do to bit a little more stuffy and rigid and in my opinion too much emphasis on the 'pecking order' of the organisation. It is also possible to find thuggish or bullying behaviour in traditional classes and is usually pretty easy to notice fairly early on.

I am not saying hierarchy or ranking is wrong as I do believe in order and discipline but you will probably find that, should you travel from white belt to black belt and beyond, you will come across those clubs and associations that exude traits of being a 'cult'. Martial arts cults are a whole new topic and there have been many, many books and articles written on this subject. I have recently finished one called 'Herding The Moo' which documents one man's journey with a cult that ruined many people's lives. It is an interesting read and I recommend it to anyone who wants to study a martial art but does not know what to look for when searching for a reputable school. Apart from that, go and Google 'martial arts cult' and you'll find all the information that you need on this topic. Remember too that not everything on the internet is true so remain judgemental and go with your instinct. If something doesn't feel right with an instructor or a club then it probably isnt right. Find one that 'sits' better with you.

Another thing to research online is a 'McDojo'. All McDojos will have similar traits and excellent ways of relieving you of your hard earned cash so try to avoid these places too. In summary a McDojo is a martial arts training hall that is designed to bring the instructor money and is usually at the expense of the quality and practicality of what is being taught.

Although I cannot remember where I initially found it, I remember putting on the smartest shirt that I could find along with a pair of suit trousers and cleaning my black leather shoes for the interview. I was a little nervous but I had been for many job interviews in the past so this was quite familiar for me.

I had applied for a job with the local newspaper.

The job was to sells advertising space to local businesses around Bedford and neighbouring villages. It came with a salary slightly larger than my shit shifting salary and also a company car. The interview was at (in my opinion) the best hotel in town which overlooked the River Great Ouse at the bottom of the high street.

The Swan Hotel has played host to many famous people over the years including Robbie Williams, Take That and Hugh Jackman to name but a few. It has an air of prestige and old English muster about it and was not somewhere that I would normally go to but I could easily put on a persona of one who is comfortable in these surroundings. A lot of sales jobs are about putting on an act and 'playing the game' with your clients and newspapers were no different. Selling ads in newspapers is about long term relationships and building rapport with businesses of single people right up to councils and large corporations. The sales person adopts that persona which relates to the client. It would dictate whether you call your client 'mate', 'Mr. Smith' or 'Sir' and how you converse with your client

The interview was with the commercial director for the paper and although I do not remember the content of the interview I do recall that the conversation flowed as we sat there drinking tea in the bar. I remember being in that moment and feeling confident about getting the job. After all, I had excelled at sales in banking so I should be able to float right into this job.

It was a good interview. The conversation was comfortable and not awkward. The interview took place on a warm afternoon and the commercial director sat in front of a window which displayed the beautiful river and embankment basking in sunshine. People would walk past looking happy and chatting and the occasional boat rowed from one side of the window's landscape scene to the other. Several people were in the bar at that time of day and were quietly chatting and enjoying an afternoon drink. It was calm. Relaxed. I liked this. It had been a turbulent time lately and the positivity of the moment was something to be remembered. It was, indeed, the success of that interview that opened the door of the media world to me and this is a world that I am still in today. Things have changed somewhat and I now work in a digital world surrounded by social media, websites and analytical data. Local newspapers still exist but they are dying out as the digital age sits atop a throne and reigns over print. Times move on. I moved with them.

My martial arts moved with them too. This is where I find modern martial arts like Brazilian Jiu Jitsu and MMA have an unwritten but ingrained code that moves with the times whereas some traditional school are still working for a society that is not in sync with how we tend to live our lives. Rather than force or demand that a group or club conform to 'how it was' or 'how it

should be' it is better to yield and bend and to move with the momentum using it to your advantage. Go with the flow. Bruce Lee would have likened this to 'being like water' as it is the 'softest stuff in the world but it can penetrate rock'.
Perseverance.
When something is right you need to persevere to stick at it. When something is difficult you need to persevere with it until it is easy. Take your time to learn and adapt and flow rather than forcing it to confirm to *your* demands. If something won't work or you cannot master a technique it is because you are not doing it right (or because it is just not the right thing for you). So doing it the same way will not leads to success. Not if you practice it 10,000 times. You need to learn, adapt and flow with movements and techniques to understand and master them.
Persevere.

Red belt in Taekwon-Do is the last colour before black. Red signifies proficiency in technique and warns the opponent to stay away. It means you're probably turning into a bit of a badass by now.
Red belt sucks.
Red belt with a black tag sucks even more.
This is as close as you can get to being a black belt but everyone knows you are *not yet* a black belt. When you pass your black tag grading you know that there is a minimum of six months of hard work before you are eligible to apply for your black belt grading (assuming your instructor thinks you are ready too). At this stage it is hard to remember that we are all on a valuable journey of experience and that it is the journey that is important. The black belt is a milestone in someone's life. An achievement that, once upon a time, was too far off on the horizon to even contemplate. Now here, at black tag, many will just want to reach the journey's end and be done with it. But with every achievement there comes the begging question: *What do I do*

now that I have achieved this goal? Remember that. Hopefully you will need to answer that question someday.

Six months is the same amount of time required to pass between red belt to black tag and from black tag to black belt. However, the ITF syllabus has one pattern to learn for black tag (Hwarang) yet three to learn for black belt (Kwang Ge, Po Eun and Gae Beck). Three times the patterns. Three times the theory along with everything else learned so far and the added pressure of knowing that this is for a black belt. You are testing to enter an exclusive club where you are perceived to have accomplished competence. The untrained will deem you an expert who has the answer to ever question about martial arts that ever existed (whereas in reality you are the same guy who was a black tag a week ago just a little lighter in the wallet). I found that once I had become a black tag I was now on a journey of technique and memory and had put aside feeling and behaviour. I wanted the belt. I wanted to be a black belt. I felt that I deserved it after thirteen years of getting beaten up. It had been a lot of blood, sweat and tears (mainly sweat) and I needed this.

At this penultimate stage of my journey I was turning my life around. My job was going well and I had moved out of Beirut Towers and into a nice, two bedroom, terraced house in a quiet cul-de-sac on the outskirts of town. I had moved up a rung on the ladder of prosperity. Beckie's dad helped me to move my stuff out of the pokey, dingy DSS flat and I found out later on that he said he had seen nicer places whilst on a missionary trip to Romania to help in the orphanages.

Our little house had a front and back garden and even a garage in a little yard next to our row of houses. I spend hundreds of hours in that garage over the past eight years working out and sparring with friends. I call it 'Spider's Gym'. I won't explain why. If you can't figure it out please put this book down and go find some crayons or a picture book.

So life was ticking by nicely and even my job as a field sales executive for the local newspaper meant that I could get out and about and steal little nuggets of time here and there for martial arts theory study.

At lunchtimes I would walk up to the local pub and sit with a cup of tea writing out the meaning of patterns over and over and going through the names of body parts and movements in Korean. When the founder of Taekwon-Do, General Choi Hong Hi wrote the 'bible' of Taekwon-Do he wrote it very specifically with a scientific approach to a philosophical art. Theory was riddled with percentages, distances and precise measurements which needed to be known in theory and displayed in practice to ensure a pass.

I reckon I spent more time studying the theory than most black tags. I really did spend a heck of a long time going over it. My theory book was crammed full of little notes and acronyms and ways to remember difficult things. Past experience and assisting with club gradings had made me see that those who did not study enough had the weight of the theory section hanging over them like a gallows ready to drop. Knowing your theory did not make you a better fighter but it showed an examiner who really had the desire to do what needed to be done to earn their belt. Here was an opportunity to reach a pivotal goal in life. One learns the techniques. One learns the patterns and one even becomes good at sparring. So now you get told "OK- if you want the belt all you have to do is learn this theory. It's all in this booklet! Just look at it for ten minutes a day for six months and you'll know it back to front."

I would say I gave it on average thirty minutes per day.

So if this part of the test is laid out so damn clearly and you have a book with all the answers in it, why is it that the majority of people do not learn their theory? Laziness? If you get to black tag surely you can't be lazy. Inability? Same response as before. So what is it? Ignorance maybe. Whatever it is it always narks

126

me when I grade one of my students and they stare at me like they are a wax work of themselves, expressionless and lifeless when I ask them their questions.

Make sure you learn your theory people! Whether you like the theory or not just bloody do it! It'll take a weight off of your mind and really ease the pressure and, to put it bluntly, can drag you through a grading if you fuck up another part of it too because it shows desire and a willingness to learn.

This is assuming that your chosen art has a theory section to it. The chances are that if you have chosen a traditional style then you will have some theory to learn. This will usually consist of learning the movements of the art in the mother tongue of the founder along with meanings of patterns or kata, counting, general etiquette and manners and some other philosophical stuff. Expect theory if you choose Karate, Taekwon-Do, Kung Fu, Japanese Jiu Jitsu, Judo or anything else from that part of the world. Now you are forewarned so don't whine when the theory is expected to be learned.

Now let's flip this theory thing on its head.

What the fuck is the point of learning all this crap in another language?! How does that help me to kick the crap out of someone when required?

Well it doesn't. It does mean that you show heart and desire to do what needs to be done and it means you can learn from any school in the world if one accepted set of terminology is used too. But it won't help you to kick ass. It won't.

And I have further news for you my friend: that black belt won't mean you can kick ass either.

Sorry to burst your bubble. Here you are two thirds of the way into a book about the journey from white to black belt and what it means to get there and I tell you that you won't be an invincible warrior of justice when you get to your destination. Well I need to be honest with you because you should be looking to know what the *journey* means not the *destination*. Black belt is a beginning.

It is the start of another journey and you may not realise what that journey is until you get there. It is an amazing achievement but it should be likened to passing your driving test: you are not a better driver than the day before. You are simply qualified now. You are expected to drive a certain way and the consequences for not adhering to the rules are catastrophic. As a black belt you now have to know everything and be able to do everything because once you get that belt around your waist you, brother, are the main man. Everyone else in that class will see you as the next oracle of your art. That's another damn good reason to know your theory actually…

So what I'm going to do is tell you all about how I got my black belt: the experience of the grading, what it entailed and what happened afterwards that made me doubt that I deserved to put a black belt around my waist.

Chapter Seven

Black Belt

There were two main seminars for our Taekwon-Do association each year. These were around March/ April and September time. The seminars served as a way to get the whole association together to learn under all of the top ranked grades in the country as well as other guest instructors from Europe and beyond. It also served its purpose to hold black belt gradings too. A general rule in a lot of martial arts is that an instructor can grade up to two belts below their own level. This means that a third degree black belt would be required to grade someone to first degree black belt. In ITF Taekwon-Do that is taken even further in that any grading whether coloured belt or black belt must be signed off by a fourth degree black belt.

Black belt gradings would often have a variety of levels grading for first degree upwards. The highest I saw was for sixth degree black belt. This would require a panel of very high ranking black belts as you can imagine and this is why black belt gradings are only held twice per year. It is not always straight forward getting all of these people in the same place at the same time.

I would also add that there is another purpose for these large seminars which I believe is not just my scepticism but is clear fact and something that was not evident early on in my practice but became more evident the more I learned about martial arts. That reason is that seminars are an excellent way for an association to make money and potentially for a select few individuals to make money too. There are several factors which go towards weighing up if a seminar is worth the cost. Suffice to say if someone today said I could go to a Taekwon-Do seminar for thirty pounds for a three hour session with a seventh degree black belt master I would probably decline. However I would pay fifty pounds for a Brazilian Jiu Jitsu seminar with a BJJ black belt who is proving his worth on the circuit and is known for their technical ability. I am not trying to be style specific with this analogy. It is related to my personal beliefs and goals for martial arts right now.

Usually a full blown bi-annual Taekwon-Do seminar would be up to four hours long. A minimum of an hour would be a very physical warm up followed by sparring drills, footwork, pad work and anything else from guest instructors. It could take about half an hour to get 300 or more Taekwon-Doists lined up in grade order at the beginning of the session!

The second part of the seminar might be for patterns. Those taking a grading might have a chance to go over their respective patterns and get some last minute pointers before breaking away to another place in the building to do their exam. From there the remaining students would continue their seminar to the end and either wait for any colleagues taking their grading, wrap up and go home or go and find a place to eat. Most of the time these huge sessions would take place somewhere in the south east of the country usually around London as this is where a lot of our association heads were based. Students and instructors would literally travel the length of the country to attend these seminars. Although our Bedford club was only situated an hour and a half from the venue we decided that we would book some beds in a hotel so that we could arrive at the grading refreshed.

It was Friday 28th March 2009 and I had booked the day off of work in preparation for my grading. I had been studying pretty hard for this. Most lunchtimes in the last six months had been spent pouring over theory sheets and writing out meanings of patterns and terminology and evenings spent training and memorising movements. My mind-set was not exactly where it should be. I knew that I had studied hard and I knew the right patterns and sequences for the grading. My sparring was OK for my level and I knew a bit of general self-defence too. All in all I knew it was time to do this after thirteen years of Taekwon-Do study. But I was not sure if I deserved a black belt. I knew that there were first degree black belts out there who were more flexible, stronger, quicker and faster than me and would probably rank higher in tournament success. So why would I wear a black belt if I was not as good as them? You see, as a coloured belt the black belt wearer is deemed the one who has 'reached the destination'. The one who knows. The one who *can* do'. The layman does not see that not all black belts are created equal so in my mind I was unsure. Yet still I wanted the black belt and my instructor was certainly happy for me to be tested so I put my faith in the system.

Beckie wanted to come with me to support me through my grading but I had to ask her not to come. It had been a long and arduous journey from white to black belt and I had started the journey alone. I felt I had to finish the journey alone too. I think she found it hard to understand and was a bit upset but I insisted that I did this alone. A couple of years later she would accompany me to my second degree grading as well as have the pleasure of seeing two sixth degree grading tests too.

We made plans to drive down in convoy. There were a few of us going to the seminar although I was the only one from our Bedford club testing for black belt that day. We would drive down in time to have something to eat for dinner and relax for a while at the hotel.

Now I should have known better than to think this would be a calm and refined affair. History should have given me a clue. Our club had, over the years, been to many tournaments and our 'preparation' rarely changed. I remember from my years as a university student being up until 4am drinking with our instructor and other students before waking at 6am to be driven half way across the country to compete. We lived hard and fought hard and had good success. Crazy times.

Things hadn't changed.

We arrived at the hotel which was more like a series of box rooms with two thin army barracks style beds in each. There was enough room for one person to stand up at any one time. It was not exactly luxury but it was cheap and it would keep the rain off of our heads over night. It was also close to the seminar venue.

After getting something to eat it was decided that we would buy copious amounts of alcohol and take it back to the hotel to drink well into the night. I was never a good drinker but wasn't really tired as thoughts of black belts and grading were swirling around my mind so I entered into the spirit of things and we started drinking.

I'm not sure what time we finally went to sleep but I do know that I was still pretty tired when I woke up. Once again the Bedford ITF Taekwon-Do club had prepared in the only way that we knew how and a slightly jaded group of freshly showered kick ass piss heads gathered downstairs for a quick breakfast before piling into the cars and heading to the seminar venue.

I was nervous. I can't deny that. Nervous but excited. This could be it. This could be when I finally reached my martial destination. My mind flashed back to when I was fifteen and first climbed those rickety wooden stairs into the dusty old scout hut and took my first karate lesson. How it was daunting but how I was enthralled by the movements, discipline and confidence of the lessons. How everyone seemed so in control of themselves and how easily they moved. How I might finally learn to keep myself safe from harm...

What the hell was I doing here...?

The venue for the seminar and grading was a large building; possibly a school. Possibly some sort of leisure centre. The seminar was to be held in a full size indoor sports hall. It was one of those halls that reminded me of my old school sports hall with basketball rings around the edges and lines painted in several colours on the floor to outline the various pitches and courts that could be played in the hall. Everywhere you looked people were warming up and chatting with fellow students from their own schools or catching up with those from faraway schools who hadn't been seen since that last tournament or seminar. Everyone was buoyant and enthusiastic which was normal for an annual seminar. It was everyone's favourite road trip in the Taekwon-Do fraternity.

In any martial art you will usually find a community of people who share a common goal and will generally relish in anything that will help their pursuit of this goal. People can be extremely positive and it is a good thing in life to surround yourself with these sorts of people and these types of activities and events. The atmosphere was electric and motivational and alive with energy and life.

From entering the building I entered my usual state of mentally separating myself from my colleagues and others. Whereas I could feed off of the positivity of others I generally took a step back and would observe how others acted and how they enjoyed their day. I would be pleased for them rather than be pleased with them.

I went to get changed. The changing room was equally full of fellow students all chatting and preparing for the inevitable martial marathon that lay ahead. The strong, pungent scent of Deep Heat hung in the air and tickled the throat. That smell always reminded me of previous competitions and thai fights that I had attended and competed in. I used to wonder whether athletes used it because they were always injured or just couldn't be bothered to warm up properly.

I took myself to a corner of the room and got myself changed, listening to the banter around me. I tied my belt around my waist wondering if this would be the last time that I would wear a coloured belt to practice Taekwon-Do again. I mean I had never, ever heard of anyone getting demoted so once you were black you never went back, right? You were a black belt. Forever.

Shit that was too much to think about right now. I tied the belt around my waist and went into the sports hall.

Numbers has grown. There had to be 300 students here all looking like bottles of Tipp-Ex with belts. There were children as well as adults; men, women, older students and younger ones. The hall was filled with people who were white, black, Asian, African, tall, short, fat and thin. The only thing that gave anyone any level of importance was the belt around their waist which was a clear reflection of rank as awarded by a black belt of higher grade. This was the ethos of traditional martial arts and it was always refreshing to see people from different backgrounds share mutual respect for each other regardless of colour or creed.

The start of any seminar would be getting everyone lined up in grade order to bow to the highest grades and grandmaster, say the oath and tenets get any important association announcements made and then to inform on the programme for the day's training. When I said earlier that it took a while to get everyone lined up I was not joking! Imagine getting 300 people to line up so that there were generally the same number of people in each line from one side of the hall to the other and that everyone was not only in grade order but that those of the same grade were then in age order. You would be surrounded by people you probably don't know so birth dates would be hastily exchanged so as not to hold things up.

Then there was Steve, my instructor. Steve wasn't his real name. It was a nickname. I've known Steve since 1996 from when I came to Bedford to go to the local university and he has always been 'Steve' to me. It was several years before I found out what his real name was and to this day I still have no clue as to why his nickname is Steve. For many years Steve has been my inspiration and my mentor in martial arts but not when it came to timekeeping. Steve was a master of being fashionably late and this was never more evident than during an annual seminar.

After twenty or more minutes of trying to get lines right and a few shouts from those in charge to get a move on the lines were starting to look more ordered. There would have been about seven or eight lines with maybe forty students in each line and the first two lines at least were black belts from first degree up to sixth degree.

As everyone was finally happy with where they were standing Steve would breeze into the main hall and I sometimes wondered whether it was some sort of old joke or whether he did it on purpose but it would mean that people would have to shuffle up or go to the next line if at the end of a line. I found it pretty funny because he did it a few times in seminars. He knew the main guys in the association well. He was one of the people involved with setting up the association many years ago and the seventh and eighth degrees just rolled their eyes, smiled and shook their heads. Steve plonked himself at the end of a line of black belts so that we could start. That line would have one extra person in it for now. If anyone reading this book was there on that day and had OCD I feel just a bit sorry for you.

The first part of the seminar was a Taekwon-Do 'warm up'. Anyone else would call this a fully-fledged and intense workout but to us it was a warm up. I would normally be wet through with sweat after about twenty minutes but it could go on for an hour until whoever was taking the session was happy that everyone was putting in enough effort. Exercises would be strenuous and repetitive with a tendency towards strong plyometric movements. I remember one such exercise: leapfrogging over someone then crouching down. Then another person would do the same and join the end of the line. The line would then stretch across the whole damn hall. When everyone was crouched down the first person (who would not have jumped over anyone yet) would then get up and leapfrog over the completed line. The leapfrog bit would be without using the hands to brace against any of the crouching people and from a two foot jump over a crouched down body with no stopping between jumps. Imagine that across a full length training hall after completing various other, similar exercises and doing this for an hour. It was tiring and everyone knew they had more to come.

One thing about these seminars that I didn't agree with was that I would have to wait long periods of time (for me) before I could drink water. Even if a seminar was held at our own club or outside of the annual seminar it was normal for a high grade to work the students fairly hard before letting them have a break (which is when we could have a drink).

I have always sweated a lot during exercise. I'm just a hot bloke. It doesn't take me long to warm my body up at all and my dobok would be wet through after half an hour of physical activity. I would often bring several jackets to a seminar with me. Not everyone is built the same and whereas many years ago it may have been good to acclimatise to training without water (as water might not have been readily available), society has moved on considerably in the last thousand years or so. I do not agree with the unwritten martial commandment that 'thou shalt not drink water until a higher grade tells you that you are worthy'. It's water.

Feeling thirsty mean you are dehydrated. Being dehydrated is shit and affects performance and concentration which detracts from the learning experience. It can also lead to cramps, dizziness, racing pulses and that is when accidents and injuries can happen. I would struggle immensely during these seminars and it was the one thing that I dreaded about attending them. I teach classes now and I make sure the children break every twenty minutes or so if they need a drink especially on a hot day. I want them comfortable and paying attention, not whining that they need a drink or that they are bored. In my adult class I don't break at all but I do tell them to drink whenever they want. Have their bottle at the end of the mats. Again I want them paying attention and I have enough respect for them as human being not to dictate when they can have a fucking slug of water if they want one because we are not in a cult.

Over the years I have read a lot about cult behaviour in martial arts and how blindly students can follow instructions without ever questioning them regardless of whether instructions make sense or even add to the learning experience of the art. Not being able to drink water until you are told is one of those behaviours. I do understand that certain situations require some self-control and you can't necessarily always eat or drink in every situation but during hard physical activity you cannot treat everyone the same. Especially a sweaty bastard like me.

Whilst I'm in the mood to be honest about cult behaviour there will be a lot of those in the fraternity who would say that paying thirty pounds for a seminar when there will be 300 people attending is also pretty cultish in that this would produce £9000 for a single day of tuition which is bound to be a decent profit after expenses. Add to that fifty people each paying an average of £150 for their black belt test and this adds another £7500 to the pot. It was highly unlikely that you would get any decent 1-2-1 tuition either considering the amount of people so it would really be one big training session. I would get better attention back my club at home and I had complete trust in Steve to help me progress as required. I preferred it when we got guest instructors in at the club in Bedford too for the same reason that we got good attention. The national seminars were more of a spectacle and a day out than a productive learning experience. Rant over.

Warm up done we had one minute respite where we gathered ourselves, caught our breath and where I downed about two litres of water. I felt so dehydrated I could have survived ten minutes in the microwave. Once refreshed we moved onto the next part of the seminar which was practicing kicking techniques mixed with a splash of Taekwon-Do footwork and competition techniques. It would be harder to lift the legs after such an intense warm up and I would rely on my fitness and youth to drag me through these sessions. I would imagine that older students and martial hobbyists found these seminars considerable tougher than me. Higher black belt grades would demonstrate techniques for the main instructor and then we would practice them accordingly. I would marvel at how the higher grades who demonstrated techniques would be able to perform beautifully aesthetic techniques whilst spinning or jumping after an hour of hard exercise and realise that there was still a lot to learn. We would all do our best to emulate them and would fervently perform kick after kick after kick and most likely resembling drunk people in a break dancing competition. You had to put effort into these seminars. If you got caught slacking you'd be told to sort it out. Bearing in mind everyone had different reserves of energy this would push you to dig deeper than you normally would for sure.

After a thorough massacre of the legs we bowed out for another short break and those of us who were grading were given instructions to go upstairs to other rooms where the tests would take place. I had brought a fresh, clean dobok for the grading and it felt amazing to get out of the one I wore for the seminar. It was wet through and clung to my body making every movement uncomfortable. As well as that a wet dobok tends to make you cold, especially when you are standing still listening to instructions or having a break which wasn't good for the body. Sweating makes you smell too of course. A sweaty dobok attracts bacteria which breaks down sweat and if left for any length of time leaves the clothing with a smell like ammonia which is similar to how a cat litter tray smells when you forget to clean it out for a week.. I used to buy clean doboks a lot more often than everyone else. No one wants to be cat-piss dobok guy during training.

I went upstairs with a tide of other doboks to where the grading would take place for first through to third degree black belts. The panel would consist of three fifth degree black belts. Other higher degrees would likely be in another area of the building taking fewer people through a more elite grading from fourth to sixth degree. I was in the second group of people to be graded so I had the bonus of watching a group before me perform my respective patterns as well as line drills, combinations, self-defence and sparring. That group were all black tags going for first degree black belt. My group was a mixture of those going for first degree black belt and some black belts going for second degree.

Being able to see my peers perform patterns before me was an advantage as I could mentally perform with them and get some last minute revision in before my test. At the same time it added to the adrenal dump that was happening inside me and the nerves mounted as my body had an increasing desire to get on with the task in hand and burn off that adrenaline.

I was relieved when the first group were done and I was able to start this final stage of my journey. The first part of the test was patterns. Whereas all coloured belt grading tests would have a single new pattern to learn the black belt grading had three patterns attached to it. This is one reason why there is a longer mandatory amount of time to wait between the belt levels leading up to black belt. Patterns are an exercise in memory as well as a method of organising movements in the syllabus into a choreographed sequence of order. They are a set of pre-arranged attacks and blocks against one or more imaginary opponents. Patterns (or Kata) are at the centre of an everlasting and on-going debate about whether they serve any purpose other than basic fitness or tradition in being able to protect yourself. I have always preferred the more obviously practical parts of the martial arts like sparring. For me, performing patterns was the part of the syllabus which would show the *desire* that was required to be considered worthy of a black belt. It was the same for learning theory- you wouldn't be able to fight off a pissed up trouble maker on a Friday night by being able to name all the body parts in Korean in the same way that a surgeon wouldn't be able to perform an operation by being able to name all the bones and muscles in the body. Both the martial artist and the surgeon would know that theory though.

If I remember rightly I performed my patterns pretty well. I mean I was never going to be the most aesthetic of practitioners and it is entirely possible I made a few mistakes but I was confident that those sitting behind the desk would perceive that I knew the patterns well and had an understanding of what they were about.

There is quite a heavy emphasis placed on performing patterns (*tul*) in ITF Taekwon-Do, certainly as part of the grading syllabus. When I used to study Shotokan karate we would practice our patterns (*Kata*) for up to 90% of the lessons. The other 10% would be line drills. Our Taekwon-Do club in Bedford placed a bit more emphasis on kicking technique and sparring. This might be why we performed well in competition at semi-contact and light continuous sparring. So the sparring and technical side of the syllabus was our bread and butter and the pattern would be the 'thing to get through'.

It wasn't that I didn't enjoy performing patterns it was just that it wasn't conducive to those motivators which brought me to the arts in the first place. Back towards the start of this book you will remember that I entered my first karate class as a result of getting beaten up and needing to feel like I could defend myself. Learning kicking and punching techniques and then applying them in live sparring is what sparked my interest the most. Performing pre-arranged movements as per pattern practice was something that I could not perceive as being useful in helping me triumph in battle. There will be those who argue that patterns provide you with the opportunity to perfect techniques and get them programmed into your muscle memory. To an extent I am sure they are right. There would also be arguments that patterns would promote health, fitness, strength and flexibility which again, would all be true but they're not as close to the real thing as other part of the syllabus.

I mean, picture it: you're confronted with an immature pissed up twat who wants to fill you in because he is convinced that on this warm Saturday evening after a few sociable shandies you did, without permission, snog his kebab and eat his girlfriend. You're out of order. You're gonna get filled in just as soon as he can stand still long enough to hit you- the one in the middle that is. What are you going to do? Start going through your pattern to see which technique presents itself? You're likely to get sectioned if you do that in public. Chances are you're either going to walk away, run away or punch the fool hard in the face. I know I would.

So the seed of 'pressure testing' was implanted in my mind and had been growing for years into a flourishing plant. I was keen on sparring. Keen to get close to 'the real thing' as often as possible because it was this pressure testing that would be more likely to give me the answers to my questions.

Pressure testing is important. In my adults class I want to provide an environment where people feel that they can safely learn all of the techniques in our syllabus and then choose how much pressure they want to be put under in order to test them. Whether someone wants to simply learn techniques, do a kick boxing competition, Jiu Jitsu or ground fighting, combined or a full on, balls out MMA cage fight, they can choose their arena and take responsibility for their own fears and dreams. When you are formulating your motivators for learning a martial art make sure you are true to yourself and if you, like me, have a fear of violence and confrontation and want to prepare yourself accordingly, then be prepared to break out of your safety bubble and be brave enough to put yourself into unknown and difficult positions. Facing your fears is an amazing way to reach your potential. I cannot recommend the writings of Geoff Thompson enough for this, in particular, *Watch my Back* and *Fear: The Friend of Exceptional People*. Geoff covers fear and violence in an unparalleled way in my opinion. His books have given me plenty of textual kicks up the backside over the years and I can relate to his mental journey in many ways.

So what with being past the point of no return and patterns completed for this grading I was, in my eyes, on the home straight with my grading and my confidence grew somewhat. Up until now the rest of the gradings had not been significantly different. I performed endless line drills for the fifth degrees and kicked and punch a line up and down the exam room with the others. When it came time for sparring I was partnered with a first degree black belt going for his second degree. He was a black guy with dreadlocks down to his waist. I had about a foot height advantage over him but he was a stocky, strong chap and had black belt experience in sparring of course. He was pretty enthusiastic and had he been in a game of Mortal Kombat I think he was expecting a flawless victory from this battle. Grading sparring is not quite the same as competition sparring. In a grading you do not wear protective equipment. The aim is not to make excessive contact with your opponents but rather to take the opportunity to display techniques that you have learning and apply them in the correct way depending on the attack and defence of your opponent. You are, essentially, working as a team to produce an unscripted work of art that is pleasing to the eye and demonstrative of required ability.

In the competition arena you need to score points or hit your opponent in target areas. You use more contact and protective equipment is worn and often times it doesn't have to look *too* pretty. It just has to work and hit the right place. It is closer to the real thing.

Dreadlock started off quick and got quicker. His techniques were OK but his control was not and he made contact a couple of time to a level that was not as I expected. Now I would mention here that I was not afraid or daunted by this but I was not prepared for what to do. My options were to step it up and match his level or continue with my control but know that he would still be wading in like a hippo on speed. I badly wanted to give him a slap but I knew what was required for the grading and I had a task to complete. This wasn't a competition. There would be no first and second place. No trophy. The loser would just risk not getting a rank promotion.

I reigned in my enthusiasm and remained fluid and light with my technique. Dreadlock continued to mobilise his full arsenal of weapons on me and it wasn't long before I was caught with a stray elbow to the mouth and tasted blood. Elbows are not allowed in Taekwon-Do sparring and I was not wearing a gum shield due to the nature of the task anyway. I was pretty annoyed but remained calm. The panel also noticed what had happened and Dreadlock was told to exercise self-control which he did for the rest of the bout.

I was pleased in some ways. He has been told to alter his disposition to that of mine which means I had made the right decision by maintaining my level of contact rather than aiming to match him. This further increased my confidence in my grading. If the panel had really wanted to see a higher level of contact then they would have simply asked us to put on protective wear and stuck a referee in there to adjudicate the matter. This would have been fine. I mean, this was Taekwon-Do not tiddlywinks. There's nothing wrong with a healthy match up. Another time though. Task to be done. Not the right time.

The final part of the physical exam was destruction. Board breaking. This was done last because it offered the highest percentage chance of injury and so to expect you to perform other activities with a broken knuckle or bleeding foot would be a bit harsh really.

There were set criteria for board breaking for adults at higher levels but this would always be adapted depending on known levels. If someone was built like a brick shit house boards would be added accordingly. Within reason. I think.

I had two breaks to do: two boards with knife hand and two board side kick. The knife hand would be a problem. I wasn't fluent in knife hand. This would be because I hadn't conditioned my hand enough for this particular break and hadn't practiced it enough. Also an injury on the outside edge of my little finger on my stronger left hand didn't help.

Breaking boards is not so much about strength but about technique and a large amount of bottle. You needed the confidence to commit everything to breaking the board rather than pulling back at the end for fear of injury. It was an exercise in control of the mind as well as the body. This wasn't so easy when compounded with the spectacle of the moment. Here I was in my black belt grading with a room full of people all watching me. They either wanted the board to break or for it to remain intact and me to hurt myself. Let's not fluff this up people; everyone likes to see a good old injury occur. We're evil like that by nature. My mind-set was: give them a good show regardless!

I tried the two board knife hand but it wouldn't go. I have since succeeded at this technique but on that day I had to settle for a two board elbow break (easy) and a single board knife hand (also pretty easy). It wasn't a grade-failer. For my piece of mind though I had to make the two board side kick break.

I'm actually a little surprised that this wasn't increased. Two boards was the standard for black belt and being Steve's student

I knew that a lot of training news would get back to the head guys in the association especially if it were good news. I wrote before about when we had our own training hall: the cold place with carpet and bare brick walls to which I had a key and plenty of time to practice my skills. We had a decent board holder too built for the club by an ex student who was a carpenter. On one occasion there I had broken five boards with a back kick and a jumping back kick. At the time I was only a lowly green tag or green belt (I had been training about two or three years) and this was miles ahead of where I needed to be. Side kick was another technique that came naturally to me and I have achieved a five boards break with this technique in the past too.

I should mention that when I say 'board' we use plastic boards to imitate wooden ones. The wooden boards are normally pine and two centimetres thick. You break the boards along the grain. Plastic boards are used as wood can be broken just once then another board is required. It gets wasteful and expensive. The plastic breaker boards are more economical and I think they are also harder to break than their wooden counterparts (especially when they are cold).

If a known difficult break required mental fortitude and confidence than a break that has previously been achieved or surpassed equally required mental restraint and control of the ego. It is foolish to become complacent just because of previous success and respect for the boards are fundamental. Ever heard that saying: *you're only as good as your last fight*? Well it's true for board breaks too.

I balanced my confidence against my ability and the two boards broke easily against my strong foot sword. The physical exam was finished. Whatever marks I had were now set in stone and there was nothing that I could do about it. The only thing left to do was answer the theory questions.

I'd like to say I remember all my questions and am able to tell a funny little story about getting tongue tied or not knowing a question but I really cannot remember what was asked of me at all. I would have been asked the meanings of my three respective patterns: *Kwang Ge, Po Eun* and *Ge Baek*. I would have known these back to front. Reciting paragraphs parrot fashion came easily to me as I had written these meanings out a thousand times in the last six months. There would have been questions about other terminology and explanations of why I did certain things and there would also have been a critique of my patterns and how I might do better in the future. I never had anyone say to me in a grading that my pattern was perfect or even 'fine' or 'good'. There would always be room for improvement. In any sport there is room for improvement whether it be football, figure skating, gymnastics or dancing. However as I get older I find that this eats away at me somewhat. Aesthetic sports and activities where the look of the technique is paramount are different to martial arts. In my opinion a martial art (which is about self-preservation) shouldn't *have* to look pretty. It must, however, *work* at the right time. So when you are in a seminar (or grading or lesson) and 300 people of different shapes and sizes perform the same movement there are bound to be differences. Attackers also come in different sizes and shapes so a block would need to be amended in many ways to be effective against different attackers. That is assuming you use a specific block in the first place.

Patterns use rigid and defined movements and motions that are all very well and good for the purpose of the pattern but are not practical in realistic self-protection. Stances are good for building a strong base and learning other technicalities. Blocks are good for learning angles of defence and types of blocking tool. There are similar advantages for kicking, punching, throwing, joint locking and every other aspect of the martial art. But a real encounter as well as a competition relies on a different set of physical and mental skills that do not mimic the movements and behaviours of a pattern.

So when I perform a knife hand guarding block and someone comes along and rotates my hand five degrees clockwise suggesting that I am not using the correct part of my hand to block I wonder how the hell he would know the angle that the offending limb is approaching me at. When my fore fist punch is extended and the higher grade who is stuck in a traditional rut comes along and pushes my fist down by two centimetres stating that it needs to be in a certain place for this pattern I wonder if he is so good that he knows the height of my attacker before they have attacked me!

However in a black belt grading you are bound by the rules and regulations of the art that you are learning and to question a syllabus that was produced and refined before I was even born would be obtuse and argumentative and wouldn't do me any favours. I could hardly argue with the panel on this point and state that, whilst Sir I respect your authority and grade, I do believe that making my stance a couple of inches wider would actually make fuck all difference in the scheme of things because I wouldn't be in that sticky, rigid stance in the first place. In fact I would wager, Sir that had I attempted to protect myself from the crack head baseball bat wielding fucktard from this stance in the first place the relevant two inches would not be in my stance it would be the depth of the hole in my head from the bat. Sir. Respectfully.

No that would never do

 I had a task to complete.

Black belt.

The task was why I was here and that task required me to accept the critique with polite nods and acceptance and shut the fuck up. I can be an argumentative shit when I want to be. I've grown into a confident person who can be a little outspoken and brash although I do believe I justify my arguments well but at this moment in time I just needed to be quiet.

We lined up to finish and were instructed to bow and dismissed.

We were done.

The immediate aftermath of the grading was a mixture of relief and uncertainly. Relief came in the knowledge that I had, for all intent and purposes, just passed my black belt grading and that it was over. The uncertainly was that I didn't know if my relief was justified. I would have to wait a few hours more until I found out too. There is an odd little thing in Taekwon-Do (and maybe other martial arts) that you are not immediately notified as to the result of a grading exam. Often schools will award promotion in the next regular class. So often people wait for up to a week to find out their results.

By the time I was done the rest of the students were also finishing up downstairs too for the remaining section of the seminar. I made my way downstairs to get some fresh air. I was still barefoot at this time and something became patently obvious: my feet were on fire. It hadn't registered with me before but the large room that had been used for the gradings was not a room designed for physical pursuit. It was a room designed for classes or meetings and for that purpose had quite a rough, hard-wearing carpet. We had just spent a couple of hours sliding, stepping and twisting the soles of our feet on this abrasive material and the friction had had its effect. Now, in the aftermath, as adrenaline was depleted and calmness ensued the pain was arriving.

I don't know whether this was an oversight on the organiser's behalf or one of those sadistic but known facts to add to the intensity of the event but it was heaven to get outside and stand on the cold stone tiles at the front of the building. It was a bright and warm day and the sun shone on the groups of people gathering on the grass to rehydrate and discuss the day's activities.

The small group of students from our Bedford club had managed to find each other through the masses and we stood enjoying the afternoon sun and chatting. I left them to go back to my own thoughts and went to the changing room. My corner was gone and there was not much space left to put my bag down and get changed. On entering the changing room in the morning I has been greeted with the scent of fresh air, earth and Deep Heat. Now after the seminar I was greeted by the less friendly smell of hard work. Still I managed to find a space and started to get changed.

It was heaven to be able to remove my dobok top. I untied my belt and put it onto the bench. When you sweat a lot (I sweat a lot) you find that clothing gets uncomfortable quickly. I remember thinking that this could be the last time that I ever untied a red belt from around my waist which, in hindsight was bollocks because I would have to wear it to my next lesson before being awarded my black belt as far as I knew. My mind was going over the spectacle of the day and the events that had occurred. I had notched up another national seminar to my experience and also undertaken a very significant grading. I mentally mused over patterns, drills, sparring, breaking boards, the seminar, the warm up, even the journey from Bedford. I organised the experience for future reference and resolved to enjoy the rest of my time with my coloured belt colleagues and wait for whatever lay ahead.

Once changed and regrouped we decided that we would head into town to a known bar to chill out and have a drink. Steve had to stay behind for a while which is normal. The gathering of a national organisation is a good opportunity to get instructors together to go over association news and have a general catch up. It would also be where the higher grades and panels would discuss the grading performances and find out anything else that could assist them in their decision to award a promotion. I like to think that it is not just what happens on the mat that is used to define a black belt. I like to think that several other things are considered too like attitude, assisting your local club, personal conduct and appearance etc. Those things that make someone a solid, all round decent person by going the extra mile rather than just doing the bare minimum to get by.

I don't know whether there is a known phrase for people who do the bare minimum to get by. I think I would call them lazy bastards. Every club has them. These are the people who you won't see for several months. Then a local grading will be announced and suddenly they turn up with a few weeks to go expecting to enter the grading and be awarded the next belt up. You will encounter these specimens throughout your journey and they will not get to black belt. Well, they shouldn't get to black belt.

The only way they would is if the school is being run by an unscrupulous instructor who promoted for ego and money. It is normally obvious to see through these kinds of operations because the standard of the student and instructor is way lower than other schools. Time has provided me with many examples of these schools. In today's digital climate these charlatans are usually outed online in various forum sites like Bullshido, Martial Arts Planet or social media sites. The most recent trend as of the time of writing this is in the world of Brazilian Jiu Jitsu to do a good old fashioned dojo storm. This involves bowling into someone's training hall and confronting them about their knowledge and ability. Mobile phones and video cameras are used as legit black belts invite the 'school instructor' to roll with them (spar on the mats) where the proof is literally displayed through action. Videos are considered as fairly compelling evidence and are uploaded to the internet quickly where they quickly spread worldwide like a virus. It's not a bad thing. It helps to maintain standards. Just Google 'fake BJJ instructor' and see for yourself.

We arrived at the bar and sat down to chat about Taekwon-Do and martial arts in general. Although I joined in I can't deny that I was keen for Steve to join us as I knew he would have been told whether I had passed. The thing is Steve is Jamaican and he runs by a different clock to the rest of us so I settled in for a long wait and tried to relax. There was nothing I could do to change what had happened and I got down to enjoying the occasion with friends.

After some time a phone call was made and it was discovered that Steve was on his way. I remained in a social setting and made a mental note not to worry about Steve turning up for another 2 hours.

After another hour and a half Steve turned up.

Someone was sent to the bar to get him a pint of Guinness and it wasn't long before he told me that I had passed my grading. I'd done it.

I was now officially a black belt. I tried to remain humble whilst my friends and fellow students congratulated me and the relief that I had felt earlier was now justified. Now I really could relax and enjoy the occasion. The whole point of this was to complete the task of passing the belt exam and I had achieved that. This was the evening where all my years of study, fighting and life experience culminated in the achievement of a significant life goal. This evening was mine and I owned it.

We drank into the night and enjoyed ourselves.

Chapter Eight

Beyond black belt

The following Thursday was a regular training session. I was buzzing as I entered the hall as I knew that an announcement would be made about my successful grading. Most people would already probably know from word of mouth but even so it was on the cards.

We lined up as normal in front of Steve, bowed and recited the Taekwon-Do oath and tenets. Steve then announced to the class that a group of us has represented Bedford and attended the annual seminar and that I had successfully passed my black belt grading and he had even brought a black belt for me to wear. He said he was going to get me a personalised embroidered black belt as a gift but that this one would do until it has been delivered. I was delighted and honoured that he had gone to that much trouble to make sure I had a belt for my very next lesson and I moved to the side to put it on.

Despite earning the belt I was like a learner driver who had just passed their test. I was a black belt but I was no better at Taekwon-Do than the day before or even the week before. I knew nothing of the black belt patterns or processes so I had a lot to learn. The coloured belts, though, were not aware of my thoughts and all they saw now was the black belt. Things would get very different from here as I would be used as a reference for instruction and theory and also as a standard against which to measure. No room for fault or faltering as a black belt!

So a milestone had been reached and whereas all previous gradings had resulted in a belt of a different colour this one was final. This was it. I would remain a black belt forever and I wondered what I would work on next. This journey had taken me from an insecure teenager who was the victim of bullying to a grown man with a lot more confidence although certainly not the finished article. It was not possible to comprehend the magnitude of what this meant to me and I had no choice but to stop trying to organise my future goals and objectives and concentrate on the training in hand. Tonight I would start

learning my first black belt pattern. The here and now was what was important. It was a clear fact that a panel of three fifth degree black belts had decided that I was worthy of wearing a black belt and representing the art and the association as such. My instructor agreed. I, however, had my doubts as to whether I was good enough. Self-esteem and confidence issues had plagued me throughout my adult years and they were still a flame that was very much alight deep down inside of me.
As the next few weeks followed I realised that I had a goal to work on. I was beginning to piece together the first pattern for black belts (Kwang Ge) and was still high on the experience of being able to say 'I've got a black belt' but to be true to myself I needed to have more self-belief and feel happier that I was indeed, worthy of wearing the black belt.
I needed to pass my second degree to feel worthy of wearing the colour black.

It was after becoming a black belt that my eyes were opened to a lot of important facts that lead me to re-evaluate my goals. It was evident that although I was significantly more able to defend myself than my fifteen year old white belt counterpart I still had an irrational fear of confrontation and felt that I needed something else. Along my martial journey I had also fought those who had studied kick and Thai boxing and there had been some formidable opponents. I had attended seminars for other styles like Jiu Jitsu too which took me way out of my comfort zone as I was a standing fighter and these arts went to the ground. I had been wondering for some time whether Taekwon-Do was providing me with what I required to properly defend myself. Well the raw truth was: no. It was not. I was about to find this out too.

The Dragon Master was an interesting character. I met him in 1996. He was a fully grown teenager for all intent and purpose but was the size of a small hobbit. Strength was never going to be his ally in a fight despite the fact that he once told us that he had over developed muscles. He was short and very slim and I do not remember any of his techniques ever having an effect on their target. He had been a student of martial arts for longer than me and we had trained alongside each other for some time. It did not take long for me to overtake the Dragon Master in grade. He seemed to be stuck at a level that was not even half way to black belt and his sparring was just a shade better than rubbish. At best. I can't fluff this up. There's no 'nicey nicey' way to this: his sparring was shit. It was shit. I took a girlfriend to the club way back when and she put a pair of boxing gloves on having never had a fight or considered studying a martial art before and proceeded to pound on him for two minutes.

The dragon master reached blue belt. Half way to black belt in grade. He then disappeared. He emerged once in 1999 when we had that full time venue to train with us but instead of wearing his white karate style outfit he actually tuned up in full ninja gear with tabi boots and he wore a black belt around his waist. It was a bizarre thing to do as we knew he wasn't a black belt. In any sense to turn up to a martial arts lesson wearing a Ninjutsu outfit was a stupid thing to do if not slightly insulting. In fact turning up anywhere in a Ninjutsu outfit is stupid. Unless it's a ninjitsu class. Or a fancy dress party. I once saw someone turn up to a fancy dress party as a sumo wrestler but I digress...

So Dragon Master disappears in a puff of green smoke and no one really hears of him for years. It is possible that he undertook a pilgrimage to a high Japanese mountain where he found an isolated temple above the clouds and spent the next several years in a meditative state to find martial enlightenment.

It's unlikely though. He lived with his mum and I'm not sure he was allowed to cross the road by himself.

Anyway after these several years the Dragon Master suddenly re-emerges and only fucking sets his own school up! There he is right in the middle of the town with his own ninja school and he is no less than a tenth Dan black belt master of it too.

Martial enlightenment? Martial delusion I think.

These people do exist though- those who study a martial art and think that they either know enough to set up for themselves and pass themselves off to unsuspecting idiots as a real black belt or just have this romanticised illusion of being a black belt but can't be bothered to donate the blood, sweat and tears. Dragon Master was both of these. It's a shame in a lot of ways that these schools are allowed to function but there is nothing illegal about declaring yourself the founder and master of an amazing new method of self-defence. After all it's nothing different to what the masters of old did.

Much as I was appalled at how the Dragon Master had conducted himself (I saw him as an embarrassment to the martial arts and an insult to the efforts that proper instructors invest in students) I had to accept it at face value. I spoke with Steve about it and he just took the approach of 'let him do what he wants'. Steve was so accepting of all people. It came to pass that Dragon Master decided to conduct a seminar in my home town one day.

Dragon Master was not exactly welcomed with a round of applause. He wore his ninja outfit and his black belt and had his prize student in tow: a hugely muscular guy who had not graded much, had some background experience in other martial arts and a hell of a lot of brute force. He would assist his master for the seminar.

Dragon Master bluffed his way through the hour with techniques gleaned from a Bujinkan home study DVD and You Tube videos. He was questioned by several students on several techniques at several opportunities and his answers never seemed to comprehensively cover what was being questioned. He came pretty unstuck when trying to demonstrate something on me, ending up on top of me on the ground and having to tap out as I nearly choked him unconscious.

This was pretty shocking considering I was a standing fighter. I had no knowledge of chokes and all I did was hug him around his neck and squeeze him towards me as hard as I could. There was no technique. He should not have put himself in that position and his technical ability should have prevented it happening.

Towards the end of this charade of a seminar (why I stayed to the end is beyond me) I found myself kneeling on the floor facing his student. The exercise would be in ground fighting and from a mutually accepted starting position of the hands lightly touching each other we would attempt to dominate the situation accordingly.

I was a black belt. He was a low grade. Now the ending was, in hindsight, inevitable but I had no idea at the time what would happen. Despite Dragon Master being a shocking martial artist it is entirely possible that he imparted some useful information to this chap. He may have used other instructors in his school to help out too. I was out of my comfort zone on the ground and out of my league. He easily unbalanced me and used strength to his advantage to make me look like a complete novice and at this range I was.

Dragon Master would later use this occasion to boast that one of his white belts had tapped out a black belt. The finer points of the moment were, of course, omitted.

Now I would like to state that the chap who was the white belt was a perfectly nice guy towards whom I hold absolutely no malice but I do wonder why he gave such loyalty to the Dragon Master when he could have applied himself to his training with a better instructor. If desired, the white belt could have smashed Dragon Master easily and that is without much knowledge of technique. If this was all about strength none of us would study martial arts. We would all be down the gym taming metal.

I would take this opportunity to state here and now that all the Dragon Masters out there can kiss my arse in relation to everything that you do in martial arts because what you do taints the purity of the efforts of us real practitioners. I still hear stories about his delusion and dishonesty from various martial artists too. Seriously, what a knob.

Still, I was fucked off about being made to tap so easily and the old feelings of unworthiness to wear the belt resurfaced. This was a significant event in my martial journey though as it was a catalyst that convinced me to veer off of the path that I had laid out and go in a completely different direction. I was still working towards second degree black belt for Taekwon-Do and that would not change because I needed that confirmation of ability for Taekwon-Do. I also needed to find out what ability was missing.

For a little while I enrolled in a Japanese Jiu Jitsu club at the local university and I liked the fact that I didn't have to worry about kicking and punching. This was different. We rolled around on the floor. We threw each other. We locked each other's joints up. It was good. It felt better. But it didn't seem to tick all the right boxes. Add to that the time when I sparred with the instructor and felt that I could hold my own against him (bearing in mind I hadn't thrown any strikes at him so if that was added I would be even more comfortable) and I decided that this had been an interesting experience and thanks for the opportunity but no. I'm gone. Onwards and upwards.

For a little while now I had been back in contact with John. John and I had lost contact for a few years until I managed to find a phone number for him after a bit of Google Fu (Google Fu is the martial art of the internet. It is the ability to find things out using Google searches and being intelligent with search words. Google Fu isn't a recognised martial art. You can't grade in it). I called the number and spoke with his father who was a respected Tang Soo Do instructor. I had attended his class with John in the past before. It was lucky timing that I called on that day as John was living in Finland and was only in the country for another day or so before heading back. Turns out he has met a Finnish lady who ended up being his wife and mother to his child and they had been making a go of it living in Finland. It wasn't to last and John and his wife would return to live in English in the Cambridgeshire countryside.

During his time in Finland John had struggled to find work that gave him as much satisfaction as the police force and to stave off boredom he had spent a lot of time in the MMA gyms of Helsinki. His wife earned a good wage so he had time to spend and energy to kill. He trained hard too. John learned some good skills in MMA and had some fights that are listed on Finnish sites.

Since rekindling our friendship we had also decided to rekindle our pursuit of martial excellence and we would train whenever and wherever we could. It would not be unusual for me to rise at 5am to travel to his place to do an early morning session or for us to drive to a park somewhere to roll. As it stands now he has an integral garage which is matted out and I have my classes which he sometimes comes to train and teach.

John taught me a lot about MMA. I knew that it involved stand up fighting like Taekwon-Do and I knew that it also involved taking people down to the ground and fighting on the ground too. This would be Judo and Jiu Jitsu and wrestling and whatever else could be used. I didn't know what a complicated and diverse range of techniques it involved though. John persisted with me and helped my to understand basic positions and ranges. I would travel with him on occasion to local MMA classes where we would do pad work and standing drills. These were good times and I still massively value our time training. John is a classy practitioner of the martial arts and someone with whom my journey will run alongside for the rest of our lives.

I started researching MMA and it dawned on me that this was the missing piece of the jigsaw that I was looking for. Taekwon-Do was my chosen style whilst standing up but it had not helped me on the ground. MMA included all ranges. It included Muay Thai (Thai boxing) which I had experienced and had respect for. It had Jiu Jitsu which I was needed for the ground game. It had other cool stuff too.

I had been working with the local newspaper for a while now. I was a field sales rep selling advertising space to local businesses in the newspaper. It was one of the better sales jobs that I had had along my years of working and gave me a company car, internet access and a heck of a lot of freedom. I had found that there was actually a local full time martial arts school in town. It had been there for many years and taught a Chinese style along with Tai Chi and acupuncture. I was happily studying Taekwon-Do and training in John's garage but I went to meet the school instructor anyway and on several occasions shared a cup of green tea and we discussed our thoughts and beliefs on martial arts.

Now it must be said that the instructor of this school was not only a nice guy and a good martial artist but also an intelligent businessman. He combined his love for the arts to progress himself in a way to pass knowledge on to his students and he knew where martial arts were going. He knew that whilst there would always be a place for the traditional arts, mixed and hybrid styles were strongly gathering momentum in popularity. For the past several years he had privately studied Thai boxing Brazilian Jiu Jitsu with world class instructors as well as gaining experience in other arts and we spoke about his plans to set up Bedford's first proper MMA class at his full time venue. It was a brave and intelligent move and I would be tasked with designing a full page advert that would inform the masses of this new venture. At this time newspapers were still a key way to get an advertising message across. I would argue that the internet is now the biggest player in getting a message across to the masses. I sent design requests to our studio and we even ran a short piece in the paper about this new venture too with me attending a photo shoot with the instructor for added promotion. That advert worked wonders and filled his class. It was a success and it wasn't long before the draw of MMA became too much for me. He had an introductory course for just fifteen pounds which meant I could go and try a few proper, organised MMA classes. It was something that I really felt I needed to do. I paid my money, signed the application form and joined the class.

By this stage of my life I was getting quite adept at being able to go to strange places and partake in new martial arts if I believed that it would benefit me. I didn't feel the need to go with friends or have any backup. This had always been my personal journey and I was happy to travel this path alone. I would imagine that a lot of people who sign up to an MMA class would be quite nervous before their first class and I can completely understand this. MMA has exploded in the media in recent years and has many terms that are synonymous with what it entails. The layman wouldn't think twice about asking if someone does 'UFC' or 'cage fighting' and phrases like 'ground n pound' could also evoke a certain conception of a violent and brutal sport.
I am not ashamed to say that I was quite nervous before this session. MMA was still quite a new venture for me and I considered it the 'real deal'. My nervous energy was positive as I cared about what I was hopefully going to learn.

We waited in the downstairs training area. This was a small hall which was fully matted with a pillar right in the middle of it. The pillar was wrapped in padding too to help avoid unnecessary injuries when rolling around on the floor near it. To the left of the downstairs training hall was a small gym. The school owner had certainly made use of this space as it was packed full of all sorts of weight training equipment, benches, free weights, kettle bells and some cardio machines. The gym looked like something out of the eighties: it wasn't laid out and designed for comfort or to look good. The machines were not digital or space age in appearance. Everything was functional and had been used a thousand times before in the pursuit of physical improvement.

I liked this room.

Weight training was familiar to me and I liked what it represented and how it felt.

The downstairs hall was starting to fill up a little bit now. I was trying to surreptitiously scope out the others and see what kind of adversary I might encounter in the brave new pursuit. Most of them were male and younger than me. The average age would have been around twenty and a lot had sports specific clothing on: rash guards, MMA shorts and spats all adorned with loud, proud designs and branding. Some combat arts embrace the 'fashion' part of the industry more than others. Whilst traditional styles tend to be quite insular and bland with their clothing more modern styles like MMA and BJJ are not afraid to realise that popularity breeds desire and there is nothing wrong with companies making money from quality products with good designs. Trainer manufacturers have been doing it for years. Companies will put their name all over their products unashamedly in a bid to be known as the best brand for the best fighters. Brands like Bad Boy, Venum, Tapout, RDX and more could be seen. Clothing would be in bright, confident colours. Shorts would have designs portraying blood spattering across them. Rash guards would show cage walls or skeletons with bones breaking. Images designed to intimidate? Or to show the potential of what this sport offers? Or simply a brave front hiding someone who might not know as much as it seemed. It was in these days that the saying *all the gear, no idea* became known to me.

I noticed that these young men all seemed physically fitter than in previous schools that I had attended. They started to warm up of their own accord and several were soon drilling techniques as if they were already in the lesson. Of course, everyone was wearing whatever they had bought for the lessons and there was an absence of belt so judging ability was simply down to watching technique.

I have spoken before about how achieving black belt does not necessarily infer that someone is a brilliant fighter or tactician. Watching these young guys warm up and roll with each other ('rolling' is the term used for ground fighting in Jiu Jitsu) exemplified this as one had to understand and perceive pure technical ability rather than making an inference based on a belt. Imagine if you will someone who studies hard and achieves black belt by the age of thirty. Over the following years he trains regularly but less frequently than before. He gets married and his wife has children. He gets promoted at work. His responsibilities in life change and therefore so does his lifestyle. He arranges his priorities so that his family are taken care of and his career flourishes. He trains in his chosen martial art when he can. Sometimes this is three times per week but more often than not it is twice or once per week. Sometimes he skips a week if he is on holiday or away on business. It becomes harder to maintain a strict diet as time becomes precious and so he gains some weight. Before he knows it he is forty five years old, has put many inches on his waistline, lost a lot of flexibility and fitness and yet is still able to wear a black belt around his waist.

A young lad enters the class which he attends and spends the next five years working up to black belt. Our example is now fifty years old and a little more weathered. He will not likely be able to do as well as the young, fresh, twenty five year old who has just earned his black belt.

On the other hand if they were being described to someone, it would sound more impressive to say "Oh John? Yes he has been a black belt for twenty years now", rather than "Oh Joe, yes he earned his black belt just last week." Perception is key here.

So back to the MMA mats, one needs an understanding of technique to perceive who has good technical ability and efficacy of energy in their martial art.

Other times that I have has this experience is when attending Muay Thai or western boxing classes. No one wore a graded belt (although there is a grading syllabus in Thai Boxing).

The absence of the belt has usually shown me a club or school with a lack of ego or false sense of ability. The black belt does not, a great fighter, maketh. Yet it can be revered in a cultish and lustful way and is coveted as a status symbol rather than what it *should* mean: years of blood, sweat and tears on the mats.

This group of athletes were simply a gathering a people who had a common interest to be the best that they could be in an up and coming yet demanding sport and were only too happy to help each other to get there.

In my experience the anomaly of the above beltless/ gi-less/ non egocentric theory is Brazilian Jiu Jitsu. This is a fairly new martial art and has a uniform and a belt system and the belt most certainly denotes rank. The difference here lies in the fact that the belt has a purity about it that has not yet been tainted by time as in other arts.

Take, for example, Karate. Karate has been around a long, long time and so someone who reaches black belt can happily leave one school and set up their own. They can even call their style of Karate whatever they want (nothing wrong with branding) and another style of Karate is born. Over time these instructors promote people who may not be worth their belt. This happens through ignorance, for false flattery, club kudos or money. It waters systems down.

Brazilian Jiu Jitsu is too young and close to the source still for this to happen. Practitioners are too passionate about the purity of their art to allow it to be tarnished. Those who decide to start their own version or strain of BJJ are simply called out on the mats to show what they can do. A true BJJ black belt will shine on the mats in a way that a fake one simply cannot. The proof is on the mats. And as mentioned before, the internet is rife with videos of these fake 'masters'.

This is where martial arts should get back to.

The truth lies in ability on the mats and efficacy through technique. Trust is given to the instructor who ends the class having donated energy and sweat and maybe even wears a few bruises (age/ injuries permitting) not the one who stands at the front in a whiter than white uniform barking orders over his ever growing waistline.

Loyalty is given to the true master who cannot just explain in detail a technique or sequence with justified and logical instruction but the instructor who can demonstrate this in a live setting. And respect is given to the black belt who shows that they have surely invested their own blood, sweat and tears on the mat hour after hour to wear the colour black around their waist.

The belt system in BJJ goes thus: white, blue, purple, brown, black. It is fair to say that in the vast majority of cases a blue belt *will* win against a white belt. A purple belt *will* win against a blue or white belt etc. Purity of belt. The truth is on the mat. The truth is on the mat.

This truth is there in MMA in the same way. Belt systems are being devised for MMA as you read this book which will allow people to use a syllabus for their own gain and will lead to a watering down of the art by some unscrupulous instructors. I will be interested to see this development over the next fifty years as the rule set for MMA is all encompassing and fakes should show up quite easily in the cage or ring. There are also many different sets of rules being brought into tournaments too which will allow some fringe styles to fend off their lack of technical range and ability. Not everyone is a fake and not all new styles are crap. It is just getting harder and harder to know for the beginner who is just starting their journey.

Back to my MMA class. The Tai Chi class had finished upstairs and they were filtering down the stairs and out of the hall. They looked like every grandparent you could ever want rolled into one: an older than average crowd of men and women. All slim and all looking calm and enlightened and moving fluidly and loosely. They carried an air of mature wisdom about them. I feel that, had I had asked one of them the meaning of life they would have smiled, exhaled through their nose, paused for a few seconds and quietly suggested that I already knew the answer simply by asking them the question….

The last person exited the upstairs hall. The MMA group started walking up the stairs. I fell into line with them. As we filed up the narrow stairs we were greeted at the top by the instructor who collected our membership cards from us. This was his way of monitoring how regularly people train. The cards would be collected by reception during the lesson and inputted onto the computer system to show that the member had attended a certain lesson. Some styles and schools will only progress students through a grading once they have completed a certain amount of time training (meaning actual hours of training time rather than time from last grading to the next one). I agree with this measure to a large extent. Some martial artists have been blasted

167

over the years for attaining a black belt in faster than average time but those judging often fail to realise that these 'prodigies' might have trained six days a week for eight hours a day for a few years. Compare that to two classes per week at one hour per class (I see lots of Taekwon-Do school with this timetable) who have black belts with three or four years' experience and the scales seem to tip in the favour of the prodigies.

I had been in this training area before. The instructor and I had done a photo shoot for marketing purposes a few weeks before so I knew the layout. The stairs entered directly into the matted hall. It was maybe seven metres wide and about fifteen metres long. Floor to ceiling mirrors covered the wall facing the stairs whilst the near wall had small, open windows and a bench for seating and storage. At the far end of the hall was a multitude of weird and wonderful weapons, likely Chinese in origin (the MMA instructor was adept at Chinese styles) and more storage for equipment and pads. This upstairs hall was at the very top of the building and the ceiling was the roof as well, gently sloping upwards in the middle of the hall and small branches of ivy came through where the wall met the roof at one place.

As I had many times before in new classes I followed everyone else's lead. We entered and spread out along the right side of the room near the windows. Training bags were put to the side and adjustments to equipment and protection were made as required. People chatted and waited for the lesson to start. Although I was nervous about what was to follow I was also calmed by the positivity of the class. There was good energy everywhere and everyone looked happy and upbeat. Although martial arts are not to be entered into likely it was still nice not to be in a stuffy and over serious atmosphere.

The instructor addressed the class to begin and we made a simple bowing posture placing one closed fist in the palm of the other open hand and offering it forward to the instructor. He did the same to us. Then we began. Warm ups with realistic movements followed by drills across the hall which closely simulated useful movements rather than general calisthenics. This added to the feel of realism and relevance to the class. We shrimped across the ground (simulating a hip escape in Jiu Jitsu) and performed basic front and back break falls. We did sprawling exercises and even cartwheels (they are useful to escape some things so I am told).

The technical part of the lesson followed which would involve drilling a certain technique in a variety of situations. Often these techniques were broken down to their simplest components of posture, stance and movement and then practiced with compliance and moving on to increasing resistance. We would then move onto some sparring and rolling drills which would involve a few people out in front and a queue of opponents who would battle under certain guidelines to practice the technique in question. Winner would stay on for a maximum of three rounds and loser would join the back of the queue.

This first lesson involved groundwork which was my weakest area. This meant that my lack of technique was boosted up by my brute strength. At the time of this class I would have been around fourteen stone in weight and I had been hitting the weights hard. This took its toll on me even though I was fairly fit.

By the end of the lesson I was dripping with sweat but had been enthralled by the technicality of the lesson and the energy required to complete it. To the untrained eye it was a load of blokes rolling around on the floor. In reality it was so much more than this. It was a game of chess where the slightest movement or change of balance could be used to completely change the game plan and required me to constantly have my wits about me to keep check on all of my limbs and my opponent.

This was it.

This was what I had been looking for. The other classes that I had tried had parts of what I wanted but *this*? This was the full game. The real deal. I was hooked. I had made my mind up to sign for the yearly contract as soon as my trial period ended. After the lesson I said my goodbyes and downed about a litre of water and left the hall to go to my car and drive home. I always like a good post lesson analysis in my mind. As I stepped outside I realised how soaked in sweat I was. The lesson was only 1 hour. Sometimes the Taekwon-Do class would go on for three hours. I put my hoodie on and put the hood up. I didn't want to get cold and stiffen up. I got in my car and realised how tired and thirsty I felt. My hands were shaking and I could feel a headache coming on. Damn! That lesson must have been harder than I thought!

It amazed me how that single hour of exertion had such a profound effect on my ability to breathe and function normally. I realised that the energy systems used in MMA were completely different to those used in Taekwon-Do. There was a lot more going on here. This was like taking my kicking and punching techniques of Taekwon-Do and adding on another few styles of martial art to learn!

My body was used to standing up and trading yet I was being told that I needed to prepare for ground fighting as this is likely where things would end up. My strength counted for something but once the oxygen levels got low and the lactic acid built up I found bulk much more of a hindrance than a help.

"An interesting lesson in many ways," I thought to myself as I drive home.

I settled into a routine with MMA after that lesson. I trained three times a week and very rarely missed a session. I also worked on my fitness and soon the weight started dropping off. I lost some size but retained enough strength to do what was required and what was lost through strength was hugely offset by a new found level of fitness and cardiovascular ability.

People in the class noticed my slimmer build and increase in ability too and I started to see decent gains in a fairly short space of time.

This was about five years ago now. I have since noticed this initial increase in ability in quite a few beginners to MMA: they are saturated with enthusiasm to learn at the start of their journey and soak up information like a sponge. They progress quickly and a short video comparing their first lesson to a lesson several months down the line is an interesting comparison. From here some burn out quickly. They lose the passion for hard training. They get girlfriends or boyfriends and lose focus. The others remain dedicated and continue to step forwards reaching new goals and accepting challenges that they wouldn't have imagined possible at one time of their life. It is this ability to persist and recognise an activity for what it can provide and to look into yourself for how you can use this activity to progress your life which is a beautiful thing for the combat artist. We know that for every ounce of blood, sweat and tears that we give on the mat we receive back good feelings, thoughts and emotions tenfold and we are striving to reach our potential. I coupled this belief with the realism and higher intensity of MMA to engineer for myself a strong motivational force to succeed in what I was doing. To prove to myself that I was the person who I believed that I could be and to prove to my family and children that I was worthy of their love, dependence and trust. MMA was allowing me to go from black belt to white belt again (although there were no belts in this class) and from doing what I felt I needed to do in Taekwon-Do I now had a tougher goal to accomplish. For me I felt more scared of what someone could do through MMA than through Taekwon-Do. This was my personal experience. I was doing a lot of research on 'pressure testing' in martial arts at this time too. I had worked the semi contact and light continuous circuit of stand-up arts and I now wanted to begin a new journey towards overcoming fears of confrontational in more full contact settings. This was not a journey towards a belt. There were no grading dates or theory to learn here and no boards to break. What I did here was on me. My responsibility and I wanted to see if I could handle the combat arena again. But this time not in a large sports hall with several arenas and lots of officials. This time I wanted one single arena. One crowd. One room. I wanted to get in a cage with four ounce gloves, one opponent and one referee. I wanted the match up. The spectacle of the event. Handling the adrenaline leading up to the event and before the bout. This was my goal.

I sit here writing this very part of this book five years on from that first MMA lesson and I am maybe a few weeks away from my first MMA bout.

My first journey to black belt took me thirteen years. My second journey to an MMA bout has taken an additional five years and I look forward to writing about this experience in my future.

I also look forward to writing about my third journey which is another journey to black belt. This time in Brazilian Jiu Jitsu. I am currently a 2 stripe white belt. It has proven extremely enlightening to simultaneously be a black belt who teaches a class to being a white belt at the back of another instructor's class.

Will I get to BJJ black belt? Who knows? I am thirty seven years old now so I may well be fifty before a BJJ black belt is even visible on my horizon.

I do know that writing this book will help my mind-set though and I will re-read it now and regularly to make sure I remember what to expect in such a long and arduous journey.

I hope it might help you in the same way too.

Train hard.

Afterword

I think it would be prudent to finish this book with some gratitude and some further information.

To all those who have been there for me in my life, who have listened to me, who have given advice, who have taught me lessons, who have been tolerant, who have shared, who have trained with me and who have shared love as friend or family I thank you.

I also thank myself for dragging myself from the darkest and lowest points of my life and realising that opportunity and happiness make themselves more available to those who actively seek it rather than those who remain reluctant to progression.

Finally I thank my wife and children for being my wife and children. You are my life, my reason for being and to a very large extent my motivation for trying to be the best person that I can be. I love you all very much.

This is my first book but hopefully not my last. I'm open to criticism and advice. So if you have any feedback or want to get in touch then you can email me at mycodeofcombat@gmail.com

I will also share more information as I write more at: http://mycodeofcombat.wix.com/author

That's it. That's the end of this book.

Hope you liked it.

Printed in Great Britain
by Amazon